ENGLISH ELECTRIC
LIGHTNING
GENESIS & PROJECTS

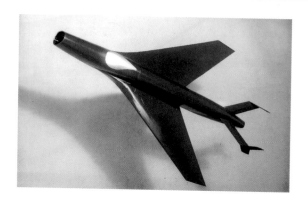

TONY WILSON

TEMPEST
BOOKS

First published in Great Britain in 2021
by Tempest Books
an imprint of Mortons Books Ltd
Media Centre
Morton Way
Horncastle LN9 6JR
www.mortonsbooks.co.uk

ISBN 978-1-911658-40-5
The right of Tony Wilson to be identified as the author of this work has been asserted in accordance with the Copyright, Designs and Patents Act 1988.
Typeset by Jayne Clements (jayne@hinoki.co.uk), Hinoki Design and Typesetting.
Printed and bound in Great Britain.
10 9 8 7 6 5 4 3 2 1

Contents

Preface

Defence equipment procurement has a notorious history of rising costs and slipping timescales. The problem is also common in large projects in the wider world. In the defence context, it has been subject to numerous enquiries and analyses. From the UK for instance, we have Plowden, Elstub, Gray and many reports by the National Audit Office. Examples from the USA include the Packard Commission and extensive studies by the Government Accountability Office and the Rand Corporation. Historical case studies inevitably underpin any analysis.

When invited to write about the development of the English Electric Lightning, I chose to focus on the influence of the broader procurement environment on the progress of the design. Many once highly secret documents are now open to inspection. I hope that the resultant small case study may provide some insight into the complex technical, environmental and institutional factors that often combine to disturb the progress of major projects.

Tony Wilson, December 2020

Introduction

W E W 'Teddy' Petter who was the first Chief Engineer for English Electric aircraft projects.

On June 17, 1948, W E W 'Teddy' Petter wrote a report on a meeting the previous day with the RAF Director of Operational Requirements and his staff. The main topic was the progress of the Canberra, but a final paragraph was headed "High Speed Fighter". It said, "Requirements for a high speed fighter are being sent to us and he hopes very much that we shall go for this. There would probably be two or three prototypes attached to a successful design and a reasonable chance of production orders. Supersonic speeds would be required for short periods."

For the English Electric Company (EECo), this launched the effort that would lead to the production of the Lightning. The effort would last 13 years before the aircraft entered service but would lead to a fighter that remained on the front line for 27 years. The many engineering challenges have been detailed elsewhere as has the subsequent operational career. Instead, this book will focus mainly on the procurement process and the factors that drove decisions about the aircraft configuration and its weapon system. In particular, it looks at how other procurement programmes influenced choices about the Lightning for good or ill. Some of the resulting missed opportunities are described together with some of the later studies that attempted to extend the Lightning's capabilities.

SECTION ONE

Lightning Genesis

Chapter 1

ORIGIN AND INITIAL CONCEPTS

In the first week of July 1948, just two weeks after the meeting at which the RAF had advised English Electric of its interest in a new high-speed fighter, 'Teddy' Petter received a letter from the Principal Director of Scientific Research (Air), Harry Garner, at the Ministry of Supply (MoS). This gave advance warning that the MoS was about to issue the official requirement for a design study of a transonic aircraft. It would explore speeds from Mach 1 to Mach 1.4. In its first form it would probably not be suitable for operational use, but they would ask for alternative designs with and without cannon. After some comments on technical details, he went on to stress the desire for speedy progress and hence the need for a prompt reply as to the company's interest. The hope was to have the design studies completed within three months, leading to a go-ahead for two designs from different companies.

Petter's reply four days later, headed 'Transonic Aircraft', confirmed the company's interest but emphasised the wish to relate any new work directly to something that would provide continuity of employment at the factory. English Electric would therefore aim to provide at least some of the operational features required after the pre-requisite performance had been obtained.

Before July was out, the companies that had expressed an interest had received the PDSR(A) specification for a 'Transonic Aircraft'. Just three small pages and without an official number, it set out performance goals of 700kts at 45,000ft (M=1.21) in dry power to be increased to Mach 1.4 with reheat and with an endurance of 10min at full throttle plus 15min economic cruise. A single pilot was specified and unconventional cockpit layouts were permissible with pilot ejection optional. A wide range of possible engines was offered, including a single Rolls-Royce Avon with reheat, multiple Avons with or without reheat, one or more other engines or a single jet engine plus a rocket engine. Guns, if fitted, would be two 30mm cannon. Airbrakes, a wheeled undercarriage and a pressure cabin cockpit were required and various loading and strength limits specified. Attention was drawn to two reports by the Royal Aircraft Establishment (RAE) laying out ideas for supersonic designs. Common features of these designs included highly swept wings, a tailplane set on top of the fin to keep it clear of the wing wake and as many as three

**Meeting of EECo Senior Staff in May 1948. These were the people brought together
to develop the Canberra who would go on to develop the Lightning.**

jet engines clustered inside the fuselage to provide the necessary thrust.

A contract followed on August 3 but work had begun even before it arrived. Dated July 16, 1948, the earliest surviving English Electric drawing shows a configuration simply labelled '2'. For clarity it will be referred to here as Scheme 2. Four further layouts followed before the end of the month. All were twin engine, two with Rolls-Royce Avons and two with Metropolitan Vickers (later Armstrong Siddeley) Sapphires. These earliest layouts employed staggered engines, modest wing sweep and a high-set tailplane as proposed by the RAE. The vertical stagger of the engines was aimed at minimising presented frontal area with a seated pilot.

Scheme 2 had the upper engine forward of the lower one. The fore and aft positions of the engines were switched about in subsequent drawings in a search for an efficient intake duct combined with a strong wing support structure. The incipient fire hazard due to any leaks from the upper engine falling onto a hot jet pipe below was not realised until much later. In common with the other competing companies, the designers had used the RAE's design concepts as a starting point (but not going as far as three engines).

More radical concepts were explored during August, including a butterfly tail and an annular intake. All of these drawings are titled 'Fighter' or 'Supersonic Fighter'. Several of these drawings have pencilled annotations by R F 'Ray' Creasey that give us a glimpse into the exploratory, iterative initial design process. Thus, on drawing EAG 1871 (August 19, 1948) is written, "Impractical tail arrangement etc". On EAG 1874 (August 23): "(Root thickness)^2/ no. of engines = $16^2/2$ = 128 ins^2 as against 50 for RAE designs. Body frontal area still about 18 sq ft. Large rudder power required for asymmetric shock

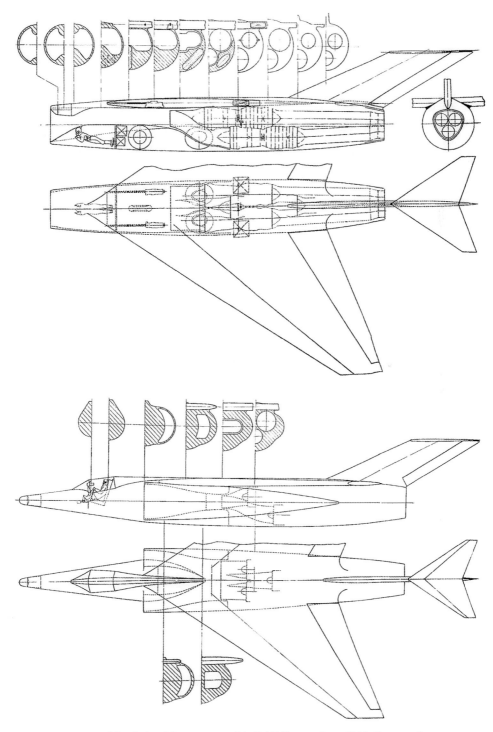

**Two of the design ideas presented in RAE Report Aero 2300, Report of
RAE Advanced Fighter Project Group, November 1948.**

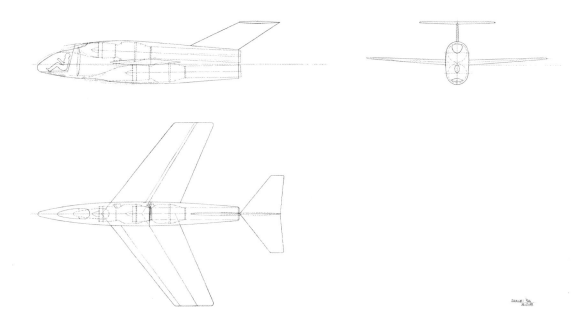

The earliest surviving English Electric drawing for a supersonic fighter, July 16, 1948.

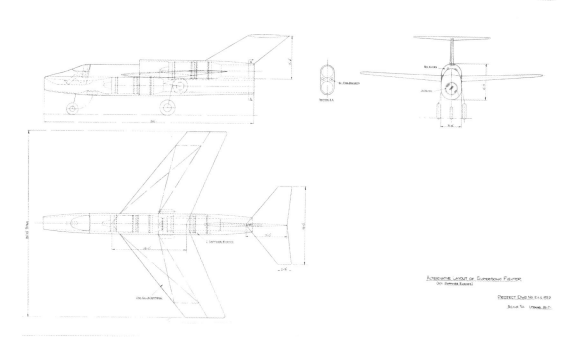

Drawing EAG 1832, "Alternative Layout of Supersonic Fighter", July 20, 1948.

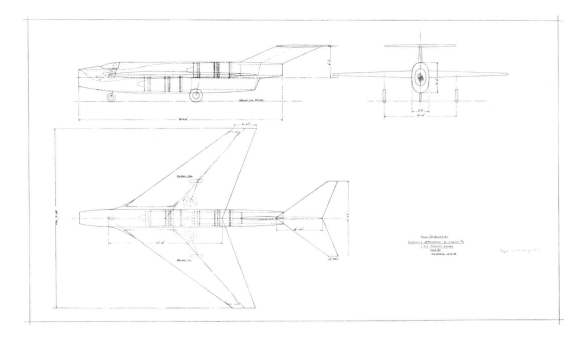

Drawing EAG 1871, "Alternative Arrangement of Fighter A/C", August 19, 1948.

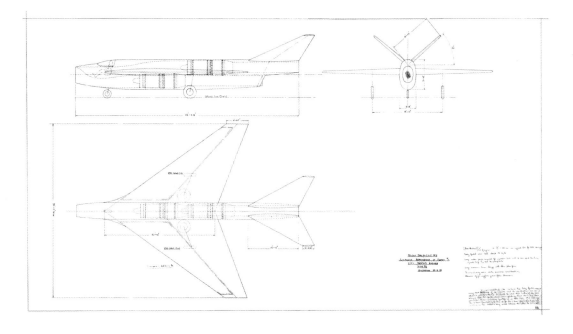

Drawing EAG 1874, "Alternative Arrangement of Fighter A/C", August 23, 1948.

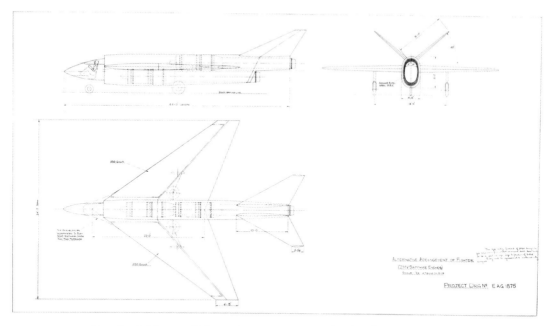

Drawing EAG 1875, "Alternative Arrangement of Fighter", August 24, 1948.

stall & low speed banking against large l_v due to sweepback. Large transonic trim change with this plan form. Increased wing area needs economic consideration. Absence of jet nozzles gives a false impression of cleanness" (l_v is a term in aeroplane stability calculations that represents the extent to which a sideslip motion causes an aircraft to roll. It is strongly influenced by wing sweep and dihedral.).

Also, on EAG 1874: "It is essential to reduce the body frontal area or wing root thickness if we are to meet the specification (M=1.21 at 45,000ft without reheat). It should be noted that neither of the RAE designs meet the specification even granting their idealistic drag estimates. Even assuming $\eta i = 90\%$ as in Aero 1960, M=1.04 for the 3 Avons (Aero 1960) and M=1.15 for the 1 Avon (Aero 1928). Even 10% increase in the idealistic drag would reduce the latter to M=1.05!" And on EAG 1875 (August 24): "This type entry favoured if proper design to get proper mass flow without excessive shock losses leads us to a practical size, shape and position of "bullet". Entry must be symmetrical and mathematically designed".

Creasey was one of the group of engineers brought together by English Electric in 1945 to design a jet-powered successor to the Mosquito, the Canberra. During the Second World War he had worked at Vickers with Barnes Wallis and had acquired the technical ambitions of Wallis but the holistic approach to aircraft design of Rex Pierson. He now played the leading role in the aerodynamic design of the fighter that would later be labelled P1 and then 'Lightning', while the chief aerodynamicist, D L 'Dai' Ellis, concentrated on developing the company's wind tunnel facilities. The team was led by 'Teddy' Petter as chief engineer with F W 'Freddie' Page as his deputy and later his successor. Petter had been in charge of in fighter design at Westlands during the war but had quit after disagreements over post-war plans. Page had previously worked in Sidney Camm's team at Hawkers.

English Electric's roots in aircraft manufacturing can be traced back to the production of flying boats by the Dick Kerr Company in Preston, Lancashire, in the north-west of England, during the First World War. Now part of English Electric's broad-ranging industrial portfolio, the Preston works returned to

'Freddie' Page

'Teddy' Petter

'Ray' Creasey

Key English Electric people. Lower photograph, left to right: Crowe, Ellis, Harrison, Ellison, Petter, Beamont, Smith, Page, Howatt in front of the first Canberra prototype, 1949.

licence manufacturing in the run up to the Second World War and established a good reputation for production quality and low cost, delivering large numbers of Hampden and Halifax bombers and Vampire fighters between 1940 and 1952.

As a result, when chairman George Nelson announced the company's intention of remaining in the aviation business in April 1945, English Electric had been included in the list of firms invited to tender to Specification B3/45 for a high-altitude, high-speed bomber. This had led to the recruitment of Petter and the build-up of the team to design what became the highly successful Canberra. Initially based in what had been a car showroom in Preston, the design team moved to Warton Aerodrome in 1948 and gradually took over the whole site as the design, development and flight test centre.

The EECo team's work on the Canberra had led them to consider all aspects of high-altitude high-speed flight, yet taking this knowledge further into the transonic and supersonic regime would pose a major challenge. Initially, they would draw upon the research lessons being disseminated by the RAE. In addition, they had recourse to a vast body of research captured from German government and industry establishments at the end of the war.

Typically, the German results from different sources were drawn together by English Electric to present a comprehensive picture of the benefits of such things as increasing wing sweep and reducing wing thickness. Interestingly, unnoticed among the mass of German research papers, there was a discovery of the theory of 'Area Rule' and its application to the design of supersonic aircraft. This would eventually be re-invented by Richard Whitcomb at NACA in the mid-1950s. Until then, the rule of thumb for supersonic aircraft design would continue to be to minimise the aircraft's frontal area per pound of engine thrust.

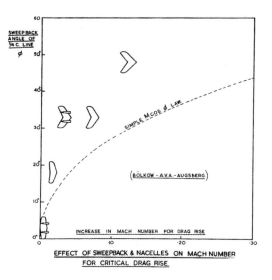

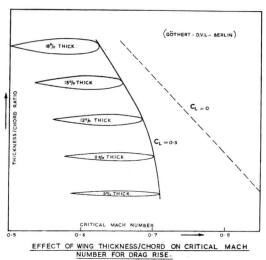

These graphs are from an English Electric report pulling together information from numerous German wind tunnel experiments to show how aircraft aerodynamic drag is affected by wing shape changes.

In spite of the volume of general data available, the team had already realised when working on Canberra that they could not rely on second-hand information to guide the detailed design process. It was essential to gain first-hand experimental evidence specific to their evolving design. Therefore, the company had begun a major programme of investment in test facilities. For aerodynamic design purposes it had acquired a small low speed wind tunnel in 1946. This was supplemented by a water tunnel and a much larger wind tunnel in 1948.

Also in 1948, and crucial for the P1's development, English Electric had designed, patented and built a high-speed wind tunnel powered by a jet engine. This could reach speeds approaching Mach 0.9—which was adequate for Canberra. Now, to address the problem of transonic flight, work was begun to develop this tunnel to be fully supersonic with a slotted working section to give accurate transonic measurements. It came into use in 1950 and according to Creasey, "We finalised the Lightning configuration as much in the wind tunnel as by aerodynamic theory."

**Low speed wind tunnel
1947**

**Transonic wind tunnel
1948**

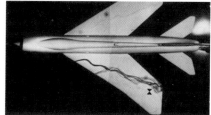

**Water tunnel
1947**

**As shown here, on entering into aircraft design, English Electric began
a major investment in test and experimental facilities.**

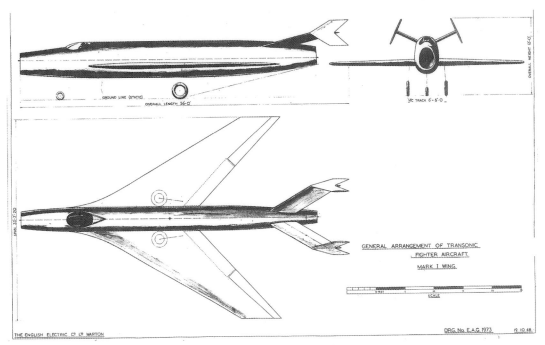

Drawing EAG 1973, "General Arrangement of Transonic Fighter Aircraft Mk I Wing", October 19, 1948, as presented in the brochure of November 1, 1948.

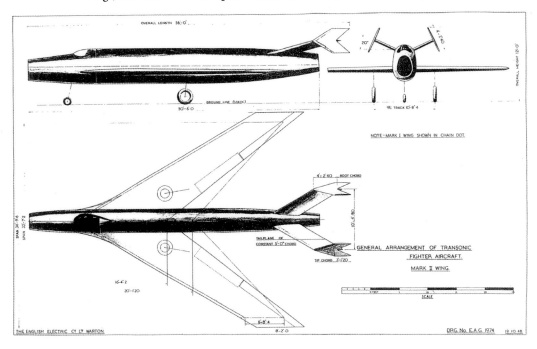

Drawing EAG 1974, "General Arrangement of Transonic Fighter Aircraft Mk II Wing", October 19, 1948, as presented in the brochure of November 1, 1948.

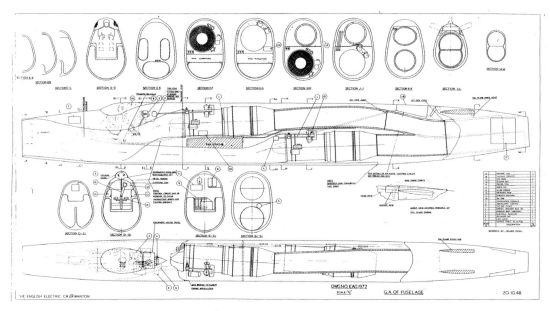

Drawing EAG 1977, "G A of Fuselage" showing the internal layout of the engines and equipment, October 20, 1948.

By October 1948, the configuration had been developed to have highly swept wings and a 'butterfly' tail with small fins on the tips of the tailplane. It had also reverted to having the upper engine in the forward position. This layout formed the basis for the official tender brochure for a Transonic Research and Fighter Aircraft and was shown with alternative Mark I and Mark II wing shapes. Armed and unarmed versions were offered, with cannon fitted in the wing roots for the fighter option together with a ranging radar in the intake lip. The fuselage design was intended to provide minimum frontal area per pound of engine thrust while accommodating a seated pilot and two Armstrong Siddeley Sapphire Sa2 engines with 7500lb sea level static thrust. In this respect it was a 20-50% improvement over the various RAE proposals.

This performance, if it could be realised, would be a massive step forward from previous generations of fighters. Its predicted maximum speed compared to a variety of aircraft over the previous 30 years, was double that of the 1944 Vampire, almost four times the speed of the 1935 Hawker Hurricane and ten times the speed of the 1917 Sopwith Camel.

The brochure was dated November 1, 1948 and was submitted to the Ministry of Supply on November 3. It was in competition with responses from Fairey, Hawker, Bristol, Boulton Paul and Armstrong Whitworth plus a private venture submission from Gloster.

While the MoS and RAF were considering these proposals, the EECo team continued to develop its transonic fighter design. They initially focused on improving the wing and the tail unit. The first step, in December 1948, was to introduce the 'Mark III' wing to improve roll control. The surviving drawing copy also shows a lightly pencilled idea for a single larger fin to improve directional stability. In January 1949 the project was designated P1 in the new EECo project numbering system and the following month the revised fin was established together with a new tailplane placed part-way up the fin.

Although the main focus lay on the choice between the Rolls-Royce Avon and the Armstrong Siddeley Sapphire; the final choice of engine was still wide open and other options remained under consideration. Also, there were still doubts about the potential

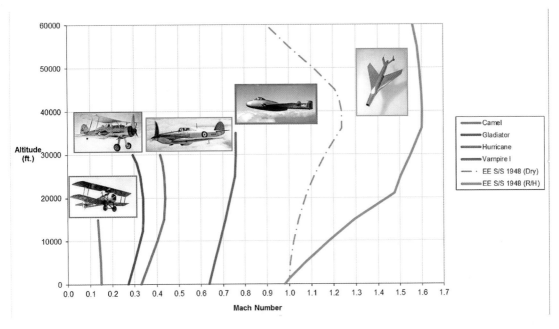

This graph shows, in terms of Mach number versus altitude, the predicted maximum speeds of the English Electric design, with and without re-heat, compared with that of earlier generations of fighters.

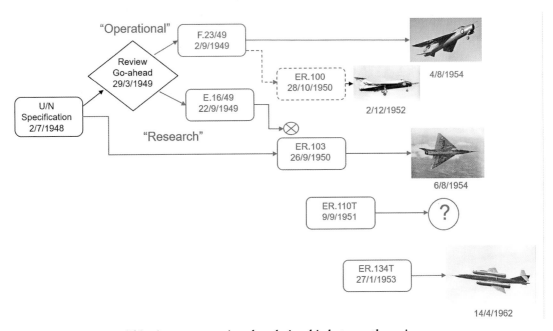

This picture summarises the relationship between the various supersonic aircraft prototype research programmes.

benefit of re-heat and the difficulties of implementing the immature technology. A meeting chaired by the Director of Military Aircraft Research and Development (DMARD), John Serby, on March 1 agreed to the RA4 variant of the Avon being considered. Petter outlined the installation factors and the implications of fitting re-heat. Consideration was also given to the possibility of shutting down one engine in order to increase endurance. A programme of wind tunnel and water tunnel work was agreed and EECo had already begun discussions with Rolls-Royce on the design of the engine intake and exhaust duct, as well as the employment of re-heat—possibly on just one of the engines. By mid-1949 the team were exploring the details of the RA4 Avon installation and proposing joint work on a fuselage mock-up including the intake duct and re-heat pipe.

At the beginning of the year, PDSR(A) Garner had raised the possibility of using a single large engine. Petter had replied on January 31 with a summary of results from a study which looked at single engines of various sizes and levels of performance. The general conclusion was that no single engine could yet produce the level of specific thrust required. In any case, the use of a single engine presented size, weight and balance problems for the aircraft design. The question would be raised again in the years ahead however.

A meeting chaired by the Chief of Air Staff, Lord Tedder, on July 12 led to contacts with other engine companies. Petter wrote to Frank Halford of de Havilland about that company's ideas for a light weight simple engine for supersonic flight. Halford replied, outlining general thoughts but saying that it was too early to discuss the project. Petter asked to be kept informed as things developed. Presumably this was the start of the programme that would eventually produce the de Havilland Gyron engine.

Petter also followed up contacts with Napier (D N & S Ltd) and reported from a visit that the company was keen to promote the E138 powerplant. This consisted of three jet engines grouped together in a 'clover leaf' arrangement and sharing a common exhaust duct. Page's assessment for EECo was that this unusual configuration posed many of the same installation problems as a large single engine and would require a completely new centre and rear fuselage, not to mention modifications to the wings. Furthermore, the shared exhaust duct could cause complex flow problems if one engine failed. Through into 1950, Napier continued to propose revisions to the powerplant that might be more suitable for EECo's design—to the extent of proposing joint design work on the airframe and engine.

EECo, however, having had detailed discussions with the RAE about engine and airframe layout on September 9, 1949, pressed on with the Rolls-Royce RA4 and then RA5 while pointing out to the Air Ministry and MoS that their requests for reconsideration of engines were inevitably leading to delays. All this ended on March 20, 1950, when the Ministry finally made a firm commitment to the Armstrong Siddeley Sapphire engine for the P1 prototypes.

SPECIFICATION AND REQUIREMENT

Meanwhile, conflicting demands from the RAF for a fighter and from the MoS and RAE for a research aircraft were being addressed through a series of review meetings.

Designs submitted against the RAE's draft specification for a Transonic Research Aircraft were reviewed at a meeting held on December 17, 1949. After much argument it was agreed that there should be orders for three, or possibly four, designs:

a. A military aircraft from English Electric.

b. A single-engine design from Armstrong Whitworth as a research aircraft from the Hawker-Siddeley Group.

c. A second research aircraft from Fairey.

d. Possibly a second military aircraft from Hawker-Siddeley once information was available on the thrust that might be obtained from new engine designs for supersonic flight.

By December 30, the RAF was circulating a draft operational requirement for a transonic fighter. At a further meeting on March 23, 1949, it was finally decided that English Electric would be given a contract to develop the P1 as an operational aircraft to a new specification F23/49 to fulfil the new Operational Requirement OR268. In parallel, Armstrong Whitworth would be contracted to develop its AW58 as a research aircraft to a new specification E16/49.

The financing of the Armstrong Whitworth machine was justified on the grounds that a single-engine research aircraft, without the burden of military equipment, could be produced more quickly and more cheaply. Within a few weeks of this agreement, the MoS asked for radar and guns to be included in the AW58 design. A new draft of OR268 was issued in July 1949, the first draft of F23/49 on September 3 and of E16/49 on September 22. However, by September 27 the MoS was coming under financial pressure to choose between the AW58 and the on-going Fairey delta design. As it turned out, the AW58 with its medium wing sweep proved unworkable and on November 12, 1949, Armstrong Whitworth was asked to drop the swept wing design and to submit a new delta design in competition with the Fairey project. The choice eventually favoured Fairey and the AW58 production contract was cancelled on May 16, 1950. A new research requirement, ER103, was issued on September 26, 1950, written around the Fairey FD2—the design of which had started in February 1949 at Garner's request.

The RAE had now lost its favoured medium-sweep research aircraft. It still included P1 in its research portfolio as covering the highly-swept option; although its experts were still sceptical of the EECo design. As a result they persuaded the MoS to issue a new specification, ER100, on October 25, 1950, to finance a research aircraft to explore and compare the low-speed characteristics of medium sweep and highly swept wings. This led to the production of the Short SB5 aeroplane (see Chapter 3). When confirming the objectives for this aircraft on March 22, 1950, PDSR(A), now Ernest Jones, had noted that it might not fly much before the first flight of the P1 which was expected in October 1952. Its main role therefore might be to identify ways of correcting the P1 configuration if it proved to have problems.

The RAE and MoS considered the P1 and FD2 to be Mach 1.5 aircraft. The next step in supersonic research would come in 1953 with the issue of specification ER134T for a Mach 2 research aircraft.

P1 PROGRESS

In spite of the agreement of March 23, the MoS internally continued to emphasise the research aspects of the English Electric supersonic aircraft. A memorandum by John Serby (DMARD) on September 28, 1949, summarized a high level agreement within the MoS to manage the programme as an aerodynamic research project. There should be no detailed design work on fitting armament or operational equipment, merely space provision. RAF representation at mock-up reviews would be limited and the aircraft would be known as an 'experimental fighter'.

The firm, however, pressed on in response to the draft issue of F23/49 and delivered a new brochure on October 1, 1949, for an 'Interceptor Fighter Aircraft with Supersonic Performance to Specification F23/49'. The wings and tailplanes were now mounted low on the fuselage. The Sapphire engines were replaced by Rolls-Royce RA4 Avons providing 8450lb thrust. Two 30mm cannon were fitted in the cockpit shoulders and a ranging radar with an 8in dish in the intake lip.

As a result of extensive wind tunnel testing, the tailplane had been moved as low as possible on the fuselage to avoid adverse interference from the wing at high pitch angles. Continued testing revealed the need for even greater separation of the wing and tailplane. Less than three weeks after the brochure, on October 18, the firm issued a replacement general arrangement drawing. The wing was moved higher on the fuselage and the fore and aft positions of the engines were again reversed to create space for the wing spar. Raising the wing higher on the fuselage achieved an acceptable level of stability and control at high incidence as demonstrated in wind tunnel tests.

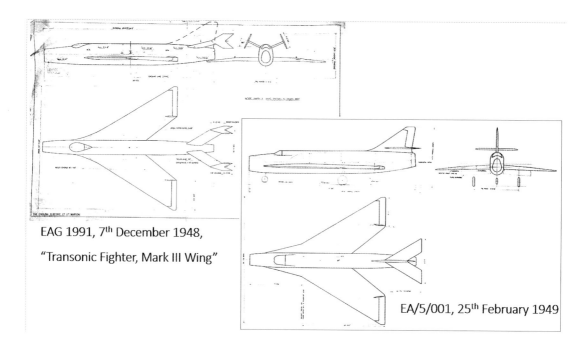

EAG 1991, 7th December 1948,

"Transonic Fighter, Mark III Wing"

EA/5/001, 25th February 1949

These drawings show two key steps in the configuration development. First is the introduction of the "Mark III Wing" in December 1948. The drawing, EAG 1991, has had an idea for a single central fin lightly sketched in (highlighted here by a dashed line). Second is the change to a single fin, with the tailplane mounted half-way up, in February 1949.

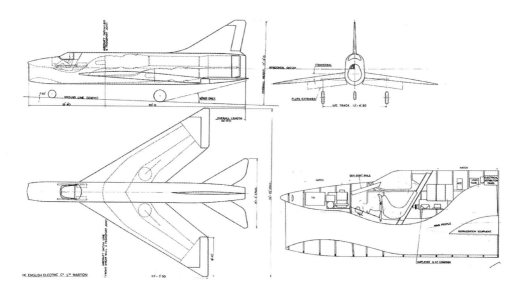

Revised configuration shown in brochure, October 1, 1949.

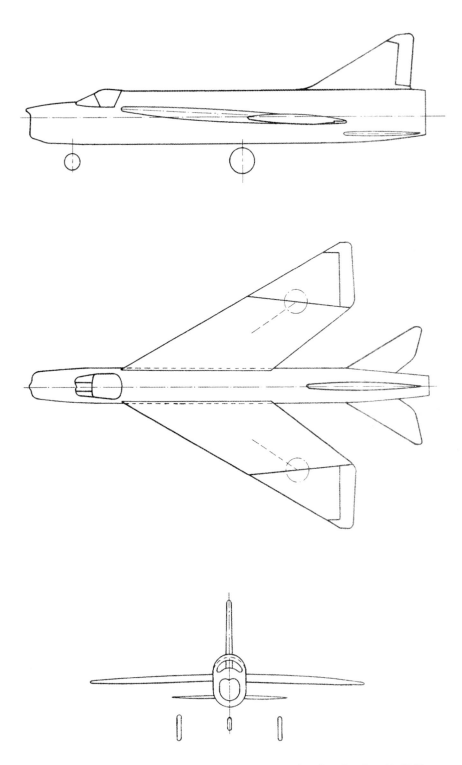

Final revision of the wing and tailplane positions as circulated on October 18, 1949.

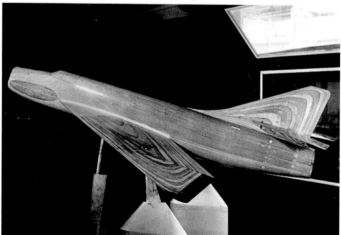

Two views of the P1 model in the English Electric 9 x 7ft wind tunnel, September 5, 1949. Crucial to finding the best layout, it allowed testing of different tailplane locations and was later modified to allow the wing to be repositioned. It is currently on display in the Heritage Department at Warton Aerodrome.

This was an extra bone of contention with RAE and its preference for high-set tailplanes. As a result, the identification of the best tailplane position became another objective for the ER100 research aircraft.

At this point in time, the now familiar aerodynamic configuration of the Lightning had been established, but it would take a further 12 years before the fighter entered RAF service. To understand this delay, the continued development of the aeroplane and its weapon system has to be considered in the context of the broader procurement environment. Note that the name 'Lightning' was not adopted until October 1958. Until then, it was referred to as 'the P1', 'the F23/49' or 'the F23'.

Artist's impression of P1, late September 1949.

Chapter 2

THE PROCUREMENT PROCESS AND ENVIRONMENT

At the end of the Second World War, the RAF and Fleet Air Arm had 15 fighter types in service (nine British and six American designs). Among these there were also specialist variants for high or low altitude operation or with different armament or equipment. To supply these types, 18 aircraft companies were competing for design and production contracts. These firms were expected to design and build airframes to meet specifications drawn up by the technical experts of the Ministry of Aircraft Production (MAP—later the MoS), assisted by the government research establishments such as RAE in response to operational requirements declared by the armed services.

The airframes would incorporate engines, armament, other items of equipment and fittings supplied by the government as 'embodiment loan' items. These were specified, designed and procured separately on the assumption that they would be fitted to a number of different aircraft types, thus achieving economies of scale.

The planning system for managing these procurement complexities had been developed by MAP during the Second World War and was inherited by

MoS. Inevitably there were difficulties and conflicts that were a frequent source of frustration to the RAF and industry. For example, on November 25, 1957, ACAS(OR) Air Vice Marshal Wallace Kyle, wrote at length on the topic to DCAS Air Marshal Sir Geoffrey Tuttle. He wrote: "I think it much more urgent and important that the Ministry of Supply arrange for very much closer co-operation between the many interested departments in the Ministry itself". By January 1958, we find Tuttle in turn writing about P1 to CAS, Marshal of the RAF Sir Dermot Boyle, "...the way the Ministry of Supply handles this project needs drastic re-organisation. You may, of course, feel that this issue is better tackled by you or me discussing it with CA. It is, however, an unfortunate fact that the project is divided between two Controllers and below them between no less than 11 Directors. There is no one man that we can discuss the matter with." A year later, DDOR4, Group Captain A H Humphrey, would repeat the complaint. In June 1967, British Aircraft Corporation would be making the same complaint to the Elstub Committee, citing the history of the Lightning programme in detail.

The changing threat to the United Kingdom as perceived, 1949 to 1961. Tu-4 'Bull', Tu-16 'Badger', M-4 'Bison', Tu-95 'Bear', Tu-22 'Blinder', M-50 'Bounder' and ballistic missiles.

THE THREAT

The legacy of multiple fighter types fulfilling niche roles led to a multitude of post-war projects proceeding in parallel, the demand exacerbated by a rapidly changing projection of the likely threat. At the start of the Lightning project the main threat was assumed to be large numbers of Tu-4 Bull (B-29 copy) piston-engine bombers, "some armed with atomic bombs". Jet bombers were foreseen, perhaps based on captured German technology.

By 1954, actual jet strategic bombers had emerged in the form of the Type 37 (Myasishchev M-4 Bison) and Type 39 (Tupolev Tu-16 Badger). Future higher and faster supersonic threats were forecast based on trends in Western designs. The M-50 Bounder would eventually appear in 1958 and the Tu-22 Blinder in 1961. The severity of the threat was raised further over the same period by the deployment of increasingly capable air-launched stand-off missiles, initially referred to as 'powered bombs'.

More critically, from the mid-1950s it became clear that, while still developing advanced bombers, the Soviet Union was moving towards ballistic missiles as its main strategic weapons. The rapid evolution of the threat caused constant disruption to aircraft development planning. Thus in notes to the Air Council on September 2, 1957, supporting reheat development for Javelin Mk 7, Air Ministry AUS(A), R H Melville, wrote: "There is the possibility that the threat may be increased by the introduction of a supersonic guided bomb" and Assistant Secretary (F6) wrote: "Every time that a draft paper on Javelin is produced, there is a last minute change in the estimate of the threat, and there is clearly a lack of certainty."

This growing and changing threat caused continual debate as to what could be defended economically. With a chief focus on deterring strategic warfare, the objective shifted from defending the whole of the United Kingdom to ensuring the survival of the deterrent force. Even so, there had to be increasingly ambitious technical goals for the defence systems. As a result, operational requirements and design specifications were subject to regular change.

An extra challenge to the defence came with the introduction of air-launched stand-off missiles, initially referred to as 'powered bombs'. This shows a Tu-4K carrying two AS-1 'Kennel'.

CHANGING REQUIREMENTS

For the Lightning alone, the draft issues of OR268 and F23/49 in 1949 were followed by six revised issues plus numerous interim amendments over the next eight years. The spectrum of overlapping fighter programmes for the RAF and Fleet Air Arm (FAA) during the time period of the Lightning's initial design ranged from the Supermarine Attacker to the Avro Arrow and included ten types that entered service and at least seven projects that were eventually cancelled.

In addition, there was a set of surface-to-air missile programmes for the RAF that began in July 1945 as requirement OR202 for an 'unmanned interceptor'. This was followed in September 1953 by OR1124 for a Surface to Air Guided Weapon (which led to the Bloodhound SAM system). This was itself followed by increasingly ambitious requirements in a series of stages covered by OR1137 and OR1145. Finally, in July 1956, came OR1146 for a Long Range Surface to Air Guided Weapon.

Alongside these, in July 1954, OR1135 was issued as a Staff Target for a Defence System against Ballistic Rockets. These projects would have a major impact on future plans for RAF fighters. In 1954, however, the ultimate ambition for RAF fighters was laid out in OR329 and specification F155T for a High Altitude Supersonic Interceptor, later an All Weather

Interceptor. In the context of this book, this is referred to simply as F155.

All of these programmes affected the progress of the Lightning. Until the 1957 Defence White Paper left Lightning as the only surviving RAF fighter project, parallel plans for a 'Rocket Fighter', the 'Thin-wing Javelin' and F155 all inhibited the goals for the Lightning—which was to a large extent regarded as an interim type. Meanwhile, there was intermittent read-across of the lessons learned from earlier projects such as Hunter, Swift and Javelin.

DEVELOPMENT PROBLEMS

The historical overviews of the development troubles of Hunter and Swift prepared between 1953 and 1957 make salutary reading. On December 4, 1953, the Secretary of State for Air, Lord De L'Isle and Dudley, wrote to Minister of Supply Duncan Sandys, "I cannot help becoming increasingly worried about the Hunter and the Swift... When I enquire I am always told that this sort of trouble is normal in the development of a new aircraft. But the unpleasant fact is that we started late and are now falling even further behind. This is bad for the Air Force, the Ministry of Supply, the Government and the country."

The cancellation of most of the planned production of the Swift with the deletion of Marks 1, 2 and 3

Numerous fighters were being developed or proposed in parallel with the Lightning. Shown here are, clockwise from top left, Hunter, Lightning itself, Vickers Type 545, Thin-wing Javelin, Fairey 'FD3'(F155), Saunders-Roe SR177, Javelin, Swift and, centre, the Saunders-Roe SR53.

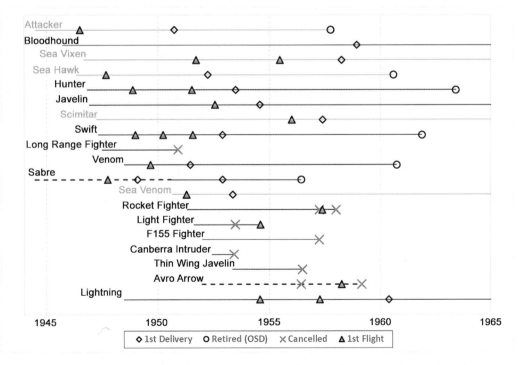

A chronological overview of all the fighter projects under consideration, 1945 to 1965. Where more than one 'first' flight is indicated it represents significantly different prototypes.

in February 1955 led to two years of detailed inquests into the failure of the project. On November 7, 1955, OR16 produced an Air Ministry perspective covering some two dozen areas of lessons learned from the histories of the Swift and Hunter. The introduction read: "The failure of the Swift to become operational, and the delay in other aircraft entering service, has given rise to considerable criticism of our aircraft procurement organisation. This criticism is justified as evidenced by a comparison between aeronautical progress made in America, Russia and the United Kingdom since the war. Some measures have already been taken to improve procurement and accelerate delivery of aircraft, and re-organisation is contemplated within the Ministry of Supply and the OR Branch. However, the histories of the Swift and Hunter reveal weaknesses in our present system, and it is the intention of this paper to highlight these shortcomings and to suggest possible improvements to prevent similar occurrences in the future."

In the immediate aftermath, DOR(B) Air Commodore Colin Scragg responded to an ACAS(OR) request for comments, noting:

"1. **Many of the important lessons to be learned from our experiences with the Hunter and Swift have already been applied, e.g.:-**
   (a) The ordering of development batches of prototypes.
   (b) Weapon system teams in MoS HQ.
   (c) Earlier flying by Service pilots from operational commands.
   (d) AAEE pilots report to OR.

2. **However, many of the remaining lessons still require action within our own department, e.g.:-**
   (a) Closer contacts between OR, MoS, AAEE and the firms.
   (b) Keeping our requirements to a minimum and eliminating all but Priority 1 insurances.
   (c) Re-organising the OR staff on the Weapons Team principle."

While also commenting on other topics in the paper, he pointed out that the large number of competing aircraft companies meant that design teams were too small and talent too thinly spread. This theme was picked up by other respondents and would become an increasing concern in the years ahead.

The subsequent long exchange of views on the lessons learned, with conflicting opinions from the Air Staff and the MoS, dragged on until a final report was prepared by Frank Cooper, Assistant Secretary, Head of the Air Staff Secretariat, for high-level distribution in March 1957.

SWIFT OR LIGHTNING

Before the major cancellations in February 1955, planned production of the Swift had risen to 475 aircraft. This large production plan nearly had drastic consequences for the Lightning programme. Petter had resigned in February 1950 following disagreements with Preston General Manager, Arthur Sheffield, over responsibilities for prototype construction. When Freddie Page succeeded him as chief engineer of the Aircraft Division, also in February 1950, he found himself immediately drawn into the same set of conflicts. Sheffield was in charge of all English Electric production work in the Preston area, covering diesels, locomotives and generating sets as well as aircraft. He was thus subject to pressure from head office to change priorities across these lines. By late 1950, Sheffield was also under MoS pressure to commit the English Electric production facilities to large scale sub-contract production of the Swift. This was an attractive proposition to follow up the success with the Hampden, Halifax and Vampire - but this would be very prejudicial to the Canberra and Lightning programmes and English Electric's future as a major design centre. Page, however, managed to convince both Sir George and his son H G Nelson that the latter was the better long term prospect.

Sir George Nelson laid out the future of the Aircraft Division at a meeting attended by H G Nelson, Page, Sheffield and other senior executives on August 9,

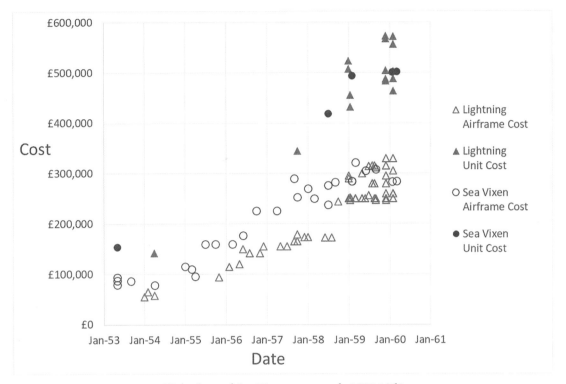

Cost

Date

Legend:
△ Lightning Airframe Cost
▲ Lightning Unit Cost
○ Sea Vixen Airframe Cost
● Sea Vixen Unit Cost

Lightning and Sea Vixen cost growth, 1953-1960.

1951. His opening remarks "described the background of our entry into the aircraft manufacturing business and stressed that it was the Government who had urged the company to continue in this field when the war ended. We have, therefore, an obligation both to the nation and to our employees to keep our activities in this field on a sound basis which requires the right balance of effort between development work and actual production".

He emphasised the need to keep in proper perspective the effort on aircraft and other defence work and the effort on power plant and transport equipment. He was planning a visit by the Permanent Secretaries of the Ministry of Supply, Treasury and Board of Trade to view the full scope of the company's activities. Today's meeting, however, was to consider the balance of effort between Canberra production and work on forward development of aircraft. The first six agenda items dealt with Canberra matters. These ranged from the potential impact of the Vickers

Valiant programme on the Ministry proposal for a strategic bomber version of Canberra through to detailed consideration of new variants and equipment fits.

The final item was "Programme for Fighter". It was noted: "There is no other development of a Supersonic Service Fighter proceeding at any other manufacturers and a production order is therefore visualised by the Ministry of Supply arising from our development contracts." The prototype would be delivered from the Works by December 1952 and the first flight was scheduled for May 1953 as against the original target of October 1952. Sheffield was to ensure that the provision of jigs and tools in the shops did not delay completion of the prototype.

RISING COSTS

For the Government, rising costs were a looming problem for all its ongoing projects. Lightning and Sea Vixen may be taken as typical examples. They were the first British aircraft developed as integrated weapon systems. The history of the official Ministry cost estimates at various points between 1953 and 1960 indicates steeply rising cost both for the basic airframe and the fully-equipped aircraft for both types.

It should be borne in mind that a Spitfire cost about £10,000 in 1939, a Mosquito about £16,000 in 1944 and a Meteor Mk 4 about £25,000 in 1949. The earliest cost estimates for Lightning and Sea Vixen in 1953/54 were around £150,000, about 15 times the cost of a Spitfire rising by 1960 to around £500,000, about 50 times that of a Spitfire. There was a lot of scatter in the data due to variation in the production batch size being assumed for costing purposes. Nevertheless, the cost rise was relentless.

The increases were driven by two main factors. Firstly, there were numerous revisions to the customers' requirements and specifications. Secondly, the much higher maximum speeds imposed aerodynamic loads that demanded stronger, denser structures needing more machined components. Affordability limits would combine with changing strategic and tactical perspectives to cause major changes in force planning.

The many aircraft programmes under way at the same time not only influenced each other but were jointly influenced by the parallel ongoing development of engines, weapons and sensors—and the priorities that were assigned to their various applications.

ENGINE SELECTION

For fighters, the choice of engines focused mainly on the Metropolitan Vickers (later Armstrong Siddeley) Sapphire and the Rolls-Royce Avon. The Hunter and Swift would employ single engines without re-heat; the Javelin, Lightning, Scimitar and Sea Vixen twin engines with or without re-heat. As mentioned earlier, the possibility of a larger single engine would also be investigated for the Lightning.

Each engine type was developed through a series of models with increasing performance. For the Lightning, this led to the engine choice switching between the Sapphire Sa2, Sa3, Sa4, Sa5, Sa7 and Avon RA2, RA4, RA5, RA6 and RA24 variants plus occasional

consideration of other engines. This regular switching of the choice of engine was problematic for the vital task of designing an efficient intake and duct system. At one stage, the MoS asked for Sapphire engines to be fitted but with ducting to allow for the mass flow of Avon engines. EECo pointed out the inefficiency of such an arrangement. When, eventually, it was agreed that Sapphire Sa5s would power the first prototype, Freddie Page wrote to DMARD, now H L Stevens, on April 6, 1950: "It is now clear that we have no alternative but to use the Sapphire on prototype P1 aircraft. This being so—it is most important that we should receive full co-operation from Armstrong Siddeley and I would therefore ask you if you would please write to Saxton of Armstrong Siddeley informing him of the position. As a matter of fact at the moment Armstrong Siddeley's have no official indication that it is now necessary to fit Sapphire in the P1, nor have they any official indication of the importance of this project."

WEAPONS

In the field of armaments, the experiences of the Second World War and the Korean War revealed the need for weapons with better hit probability and higher lethality. Larger calibre guns, salvoes of free-flight rockets and guided missiles were investigated. British development of air-to-air guided weapons began with the Red Hawk programme in 1947. This aimed sensibly at an ability to attack a target from any direction. Autonomous radar guidance seemed the logical route but proved challenging with existing technology.

This led in 1949 to the launch of a less ambitious tail-chase weapon, initially specifying a homing weapon (Pink Hawk) but later relaxing the guidance options (Blue Sky). This became the Fairey Fireflash, a beam riding weapon that required the fighter to maintain an accurate tracking solution throughout the flight of the missile. It was assumed that this could be developed rapidly to service entry. By 1951, however, research into infra-red detection had shown that a rear-hemisphere infra-red homing system might be possible. A second tail-chase weapon

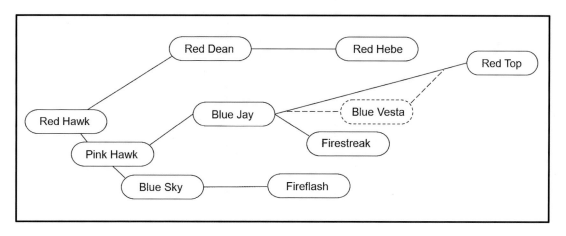

Air-to-air missile programmes, 1947-1957.

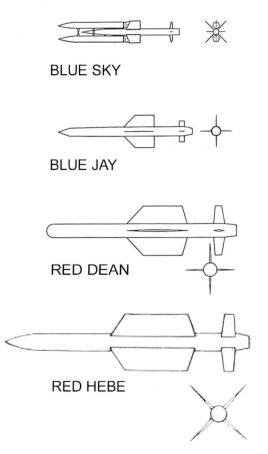

**Key air-to-air missiles, 1949-1957,
showing their relative size.**

project (Blue Jay) was begun. This would be an autonomous weapon using an infra-red seeker to home on the hot jet-pipe of its target. It would become the de Havilland Firestreak. The development of the Fireflash proved more protracted than expected. As a result, the gap between the anticipated service entry dates became so narrow that Firestreak, with its greater tactical freedom, was chosen as the preferred operational missile in 1954.

Meanwhile, the benefits of earlier interception achievable with head-on engagements meant that the search for an all-aspect weapon continued. Red Hawk led to Red Dean. Fifty percent bigger than Firestreak and twice as heavy, it had an active pulsed radar seeker whose development ultimately proved intractable. It was cancelled in 1956 along with the Thin-wing Javelin, its intended platform. In 1954 an even larger and heavier weapon was specified for the F155 fighter; this would emerge from the Red Dean programme as Red Hebe. It in turn was cancelled in 1957 along with the F155.

The only other British AAM option for collision course interception was a proposed development of Blue Jay using a seeker operating at longer infrared wavelengths. It would allow homing against enigne exhaust plumes or the hot skin of supersonic aircraft. This would be known as Blue Jay Mk IV, later Blue Vesta and finally Red Top. It was proposed for Lightning in 1956 and went into service on Lightning and Sea Vixen in 1964.

RADAR DEVELOPMENT

In the midst of this weapon development, in 1951, DDOR5 produced a report pointing out that none of the discussions on AI (Air Interception) radar were making any provision for the introduction of guided missiles. He suggested action to be taken in respect of Blue Sky and Red Dean for both day and night fighters. One of his main recommendations was that all future single-seat fighters should be fitted with an AI radar and a collision course computer.

Between 1950 and 1953 however, AI policy was concerned entirely with night fighters. The main focus was on the Javelin and the Sea Vixen yet the British AI programme was struggling. After the successful introduction of the spiral-scanning AI VIII in 1943, efforts to build on this had faltered. AI 9 was a failure and most British late-war and post-war night fighters were equipped with AI 10, a variant of the American SCR-720. The next major step, AI 17 derived from AI 9, was also a disappointment—but it was nevertheless pressed into service on early Javelins.

In the interim, late Meteor and Venom night fighters had been equipped with another American radar, AN/APS-57, as AI 21. Hope now rested on a completely new development, AI 18. This was intended for Javelin and Sea Vixen, but as of December 1951 the operational requirement had not even been finalised and service introduction was not expected before 1957. In December 1951, the Chief of Air Staff Sir John Slessor and Vice Chief of Air Staff Sir Ralph Cochrane jointly wrote to the Air Council: "British industry has not produced a successful AI radar since the earliest marks which were used during the first half of the war." This led to the search for another American AI as an interim solution.

Thus the next Javelin variant was fitted with AN/APQ-43 under the designation AI 22. In 1953 it was decided that all subsequent marks of Javelin would use either AI 17 or AI 22 since AI 18, once available, could not be retrofitted to replace either of these sets economically. AI 18 would instead be employed on the Thin-wing Javelin. In case of delay in the development of AI 18, an X-band version of AI 17 was initiated as an interim fit designated AI 17X and later AI 19. The RAF cancelled its requirement for AI 18 with the termination of the Thin-wing Javelin in 1956 but the system did go into service with the Royal Navy's Sea Vixen in 1957. A requirement, OR3576, for a larger, more advanced AI was issued alongside OR329 for the F155 Mach 2 Fighter, but cancelled with that programme in 1957.

The early issues of OR268 were for a day fighter, but the problems of high-speed interception soon led to discussion of the benefit of an AI radar. At the Advisory Design Conference (ADC) on April 7, 1953, Freddie Page asked for consideration of a proper AI for the P1 since Radar Ranging Mk3 was inadequate. Consequently, in July 1953 an operational requirement, OR3563, was issued for an AI suitable for single seat fighters, specifically F23/49, to be available by 1958.

In December 1953, Ferranti produced a thorough analytical response with a proposed design that would become the basis of AI 23. Given the 1958 in-service date, however, there was now a perceived need for an earlier single-seat AI and in July 1954 requirement OR3572 was issued. It was intended for the N113 and Type 545 aircraft and as an interim for F23/49 in the event of a delay to the Ferranti AI 23 system. This was written around another spiral-scan system being developed for TRE as AI 20 'Spiral Scan' by E K Cole based on their experience with earlier AI radars and the Ranging Radar series.

The fluidity of all the above programmes was the major reason for continual revisions of OR268 and F23/49, but there were similar developments in many other areas that also influenced the evolution of the design. Among these were powered controls, navigation and communication systems, auto pilots, ejector seats and brake parachutes. Their separate specification, procurement and technical management continued to complicate the design process.

Against the above background, the design of the P1 went through a protracted series of revisions from which it emerged as the first British integrated weapon system.

Chapter 3

CONFIGURATION DEVELOPMENT

Following its first response to the draft issue of F23/49 in October 1949, work continued at English Electric with an initial emphasis on confirming the wing and tailplane layout and later focusing on airframe and engine integration. The latter aspect would also be influenced increasingly by armament and military equipment considerations.

Although the design team were convinced that they had arrived at the best airframe layout, the RAE's experts still had reservations, especially about its low speed handling characteristics. The MoS decided that an additional P1 prototype dedicated to low speed handling would be unnecessarily expensive and proposed the building of a cheaper alternative. Short Bros was chosen as the contractor and in early 1950 there was a series of meetings to clarify the objectives for this aircraft.

It was agreed that it was intended to explore the low speed behaviour of P1's highly swept wing. In addition, it would have either adjustable wing sweep or the ability to fit alternative wings of reduced sweep if necessary. There was then an exchange of information between EECo and Shorts to ensure that the aeroplane would be adequately representative

of the P1 configuration. It was believed that the P1 would fly around October 1952 and that the Shorts aircraft might not fly much before then. Nevertheless, it could provide useful information to guide any configuration changes that might prove necessary.

A formal specification, ER100, was issued on October 28, 1950. Leaning towards the RAE's preferences, this specified an initial configuration with 50° sweep, full span leading edge flaps and a high-set tailplane. The second configuration would be 60° sweep, full span leading edge flaps and a high tailplane. This was the configuration that the RAE believed would cure the problems it foresaw for the English Electric design. Third would come the P1 layout with 60° sweep, small inboard leading edge flaps and a low-set tailplane. Finally, it would fly with even greater wing sweep of 70° and return to a high tailplane.

Meanwhile, confident in the general layout, EECo pressed on. A contract for the first two prototypes was awarded on April 1, 1950. The first formal issue of F23/49 came on April 4; an advance copy was received by EECo on April 25 and the contractual copies on May 5. Design effort for the production drawings now passed from the Project Office to the

F W 'Freddie' Page who succeeded Teddy Petter as Chief Engineer.

main Drawing Office. At the first Advisory Design Conference on November 24, 1949, it had been reiterated that there would be no detailed design of the installation of operational equipment, merely appropriate space provision. Moreover, it was emphasised that there was no operational requirement for fitting an AI radar, only a simple ranging radar and gun armament. Nevertheless, when the first amendment of F23/49 was received on June 2, it included a comment that there might be a future requirement for free-flight rocket armament as well as guns.

ENGLISH ELECTRIC P3

After almost a year's diversion to work on Canberra developments, in early 1951 the project office designers turned their attention to the task of fitting operational equipment in the P1 while maintaining or improving the performance of the air intake. To provide more equipment space, they proposed a solution that was so radical as to be given a new project number, P3. This involved moving the intake to the sides of the fuselage, leaving the full volume of the nose for sensors and weapons. To keep the frontal area small, the intakes suggested were based on a NACA flush intake design, but there were serious doubts as to their efficiency, especially at supersonic speeds.

An intensive programme of high-speed wind tunnel tests began. Given the potential benefits of this development, the Air Staff deferred the issue of the next revision of OR268 pending the results of the study.

Initial exploration of future equipment requirements began on April 25, 1951, with a visit to Warton by RDQ(F) personnel. Many ideas of possible equipment were discussed. With regard to radar, it was noted that ranging radar was to be developed to support the Blue Sky missile. This was likely to be among future rocket weapon options. There were currently no AI options other than AI 17 and AN/APQ-43 and these night fighter AIs required operation by a second crew member.

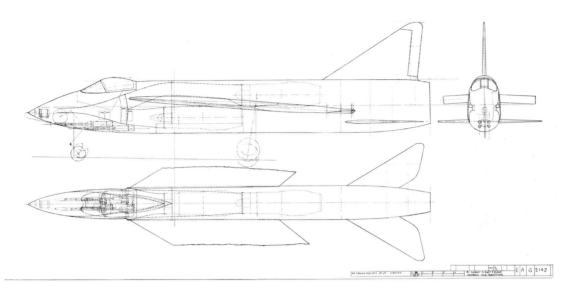

**Drawing EAG 2142 "P1 Aircraft to Spec'n F23/49, Proposed Nose Modification",
March 20, 1952. This design would be re-numbered as P3. The drawing shows the
flush side intakes, four cannon in the lower nose and a ranging radar.**

On July 2, Freddie Page sent a drawing of P3 to DMARD, now Arthur Woodward-Nutt, with a request for advice on the planned equipment to be fitted in the new nose. A meeting was arranged for July 11 to move things forward. At this meeting, DOR(A) and DOR(B) said that, looking forward to 1957/59, it was difficult to predict the equipment required as the aircraft's role would not be settled for two or three months. Initially it would be a day interceptor as per the specification. Later, assuming a need to operate against fighters, it would require two or four Aden cannon plus a lock-on fire control system.

A battery of air-to-air rockets would be a useful addition against bombers. As to guided weapons, these were likely to be of the homing variety but no particulars could be given yet. Page commented that supersonic external carriage would be impractical if they were on the lines of those currently being developed. On the question of radar, MoS introduced consideration of the Hughes E4 fire control system (AN/APG-57 radar plus AN/APA-84 computer) and its planned development, E6, as a pilot-operated radar.

EECo believed that the 22in diameter dish could be accommodated. Six months later, on December 31, the firm was notified that the Hughes E4 was no longer being considered for fitment to British aircraft.

GROWING CONCERN

The problem of equipment planning lingered on. There was concern across industry about the growing weight and cost implications of emerging demands. In July 1951, a meeting was called between representatives from the major fighter design companies, the Air and Naval Staff, the Ministry of Supply and the Research Establishments. It was sparked by a note from Sidney Camm which, taking a Hunter type of aircraft as an example, showed the dramatic cumulative rise in weight and inevitable loss in performance that resulted from the addition of various items of equipment to the basic design.

A follow up note from the chief designer at Glosters listed aspects of the procurement process that contributed to the problem. Freddie Page added a note enlarging on Camm's analysis and introducing other factors relating to the operational requirement.

D L 'Dai' Ellis who, as Chief of Aerodynamics, was responsible for the development of the wind tunnel facilities that played a vital part in the development of the Lightning.

The supersonic wind tunnel driven by a Rolls-Royce Nene jet engine.

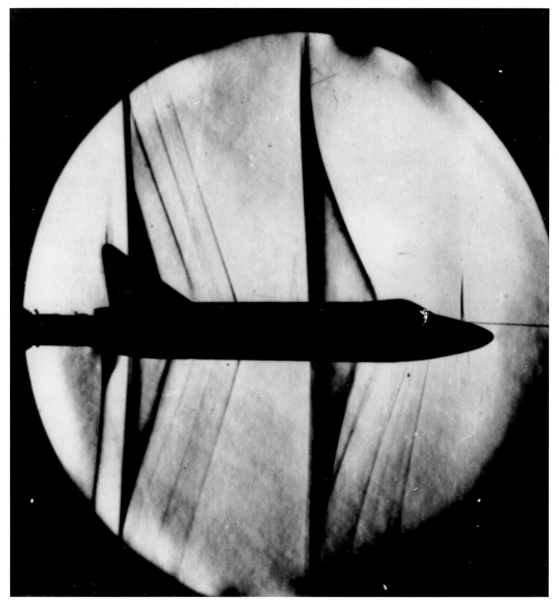

**A 'Schlieren' photograph of a Lightning model in the wind tunnel at about
the speed of sound showing the shock waves forming.**

He noted that the problem came down to reconciling the three-way conflict between performance, equipment and cost. He ended: "To arrive at any conclusion as to what equipment should be specified, it is essential that data regarding the probability of a kill with various types of armament and sighting equipment, the wastage rates with and without navigational and blind landing aids and the probability of engaging the target with varying performance and aids etc. should be available. To analyse such data and arrive at a conclusion would be a formidable task. So far as we are aware, attempts have been made to analyse various portions of this field, and it would be interesting to know whether any attempts have been or are being made to cover the whole field."

The meeting was held on August 8. There was a wide ranging candid airing of views and both the technical issues and dissatisfaction with the procurement process were addressed. (Camm's comment that industry had never produced a 'winner' by working to a Ministry Specification disappeared between the draft and final official minutes.) In conclusion it was agreed to consider ways that designers could be consulted earlier in the requirement and specification process; also to investigate the practicality of ensuring that designers' criticisms of specifications were considered and the associated operational requirements reviewed ahead of any Advisory Design Conference. The RAE would review the need for a number of specific items of equipment and the designers were invited to submit criticisms of specifications.

Later in the year, the subject of design for serviceability raised its head. EECo received the minutes of a Ministry meeting held on October 8, 1951. Director Servicing Research and Development (DSRD) Air Commodore George Rhind complained that the ADC had been his only opportunity to give advice on the topic. He was concerned that F23/49 would enter service without adequate facilities for servicing. DMARD said that he would welcome advice from DSRD but that it was essential to differentiate between research aircraft and operational types. In his opinion it was unlikely that an aircraft closely resembling the F23 would ever go into service. Discussion of the history and status of the project ensued. In the end it was agreed that the normal sequence of servicing conferences which had not yet been planned would indeed now go ahead. It was stressed, however, that any requirement that conflicted with the aircraft flying at supersonic speeds must be ignored. Furthermore, at a subsequent meeting at Warton on October 30, it was agreed that the mock-up conference would not be held until design work on the first unequipped prototype was completed.

At the same meeting questions were raised about various items of equipment: brake parachute, pitot head, flight instruments, windscreen and ejector seat. There were particular concerns about availability of Government supplied items. It was also noted that the MoS had given no priority to the prototype as regards materials. As a result, deliveries of forgings, castings and special steels were very poor and likely to be a limiting factor for the first flight.

PLANNING AHEAD

While the design of the first prototype progressed, attention returned to plans for the longer term. On January 9, 1952, a meeting was held to consider the need to order more prototypes and, if more were needed, how many and of what design. All agreed that more prototypes were needed to complete the flight testing and tactical evaluation in a timely manner; although EECo's representatives were more confident than those of the RAE about the available wind tunnel results and believed that less flight research was needed than had been proposed by the RAE.

As to the design, the Air Force believed that, in order to fit four guns and all the equipment envisaged it would need the new nose with side intakes. The company confirmed that model tests at transonic and supersonic speeds were under way and they were confident that final proposals for the side intake version would be available by March. DOR said that the operational aircraft would benefit from additional armament and other items of normal fighter equipment. Any rewrite of OR268 was being deferred until the success of the side intake was known. Furthermore, the situation was complicated by the inability to define what armament would be required in the 1957/59 timeframe.

The meeting concluded that it was desirable to order three additional prototypes. They should be configured to carry four 30mm cannon plus essential operational equipment. These prototypes would be required for both research and development testing to a detailed programme to be decided later. A requisition would be raised for an ITP and a specification prepared.

During January the inadequacy of the side intake seems to have emerged and alternatives were considered. During a visit to Warton on January 31, DOR(A) Air Commodore Harold Satterly expressed a desire for mixed gun and rocket armament: a minimum of 50 air-to-air rockets plus two 30mm Aden cannon and preferably 72 rockets plus four guns. This led to a work plan for February to produce a design armed with at least 50 air-to-air rockets and two 30mm cannon together with a radar with an 18in scanner. Page suggested an 'Oswaldisch' type nose intake with a central bullet that could house the radar. They should aim to have a model ready for tunnel tests by February 15.

On February 29, the MoS requested a rough estimate of costs for the three extra prototypes so that contracting could proceed. It noted that the January 9 meeting had favoured the side intake design but the form of the aircraft to be built would not be decided until the firm's brochure was received, hopefully in March. The RTO drafted a reply for the firm on March 7, saying that the information could not be provided until the technical policy had been formulated. A follow-up request on May 16 received a reply with a provisional estimate of £800,000 to cover all costs including the extra jigs and tools requested. A brochure was being prepared.

ENGLISH ELECTRIC P5 AND P1B

During this time, work had continued to find an improved engine installation together with provision for the increased armament demands. As well as exploring intake options, there was a brief look at a design with a single large engine (Rolls-Royce RA12 with 2000°K reheat), given a new project number, P5. This offered an easier four-gun installation but had some performance deficiencies. Meeting notes dated May 22 reported a detailed discussion of all the various design options with the MoS and RAE.

EECo then submitted its detailed brochure, dated June 18, 1952, which presented the proposed revised configuration for the third and subsequent prototypes. It finally dismissed the side intake option and focused entirely on a new nose intake with a conical centrebody. This revised configuration was given the designation P1B, while the first two prototypes became P1A. The difference was entirely in the nose area up to the transport joint just aft of the cockpit.

The new intake system improved the supersonic thrust, raising the maximum speed from Mach 1.56 to Mach 1.68 in spite of its increased weight. As well as improving the intake efficiency, the conical centrebody provided a suitable housing for the specified ranging radar. It was noted that it could accommodate a future larger AI radar. As shown, the scheme provided for alternative armament of either four Aden guns or two guns plus a retractable battery of 30 2in rockets. The text also mentioned a third option of two guns plus two Blue Jay missiles. The radars associated with each of these options were: Radar Ranging Mk 1 with an 8in dish, Radar Ranging Mk 1 with a 10in dish and Radar Ranging Mk 2.

The layout also introduced a new bubble canopy design. This was one of the essential features stressed at a CFE review with industry of all fighter projects on May 8/9 and was based on recent experience in the Korean War. The CFE review also called for an emphasis on high altitude performance and increased firepower in both rate and weight of fire. The need for an AI radar on the supersonic fighter was played down on the grounds that typical visual detection ranges of five miles without contrails and 12 miles with contrails would be adequate for a fighter under ground control.

A June 1952 drawing, showing the initial idea for the carriage of Blue Jay, also showed the first proposal for a slipper tank to increase the fuel volume by 300 gals (an extra 50%).

PROTOTYPES

At this point, something approaching the final design of the Lightning can be seen but much detailed work remained to be done. In a covering letter to ACAS(OR), Geoffrey Tuttle, on July 23, Freddie Page wrote: "As you know, these proposals are not based on any definite specification but really

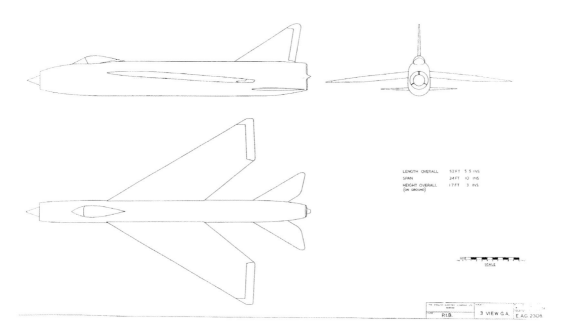

The initial layout for P1B as shown in Brochure 12, June 18, 1952. Note the bubble canopy.

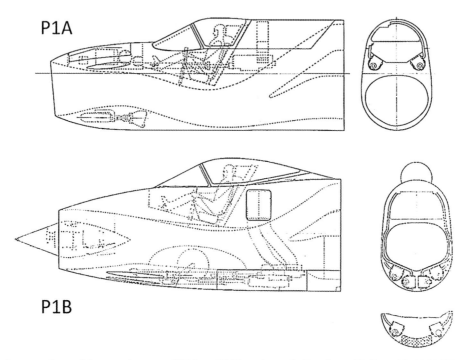

A comparison of the nose layouts of P1A and P1B as shown in Brochure 12, June 18, 1952. Note
the two-gun armament of P1A and the four-gun or two-gun plus rockets options for P1B.

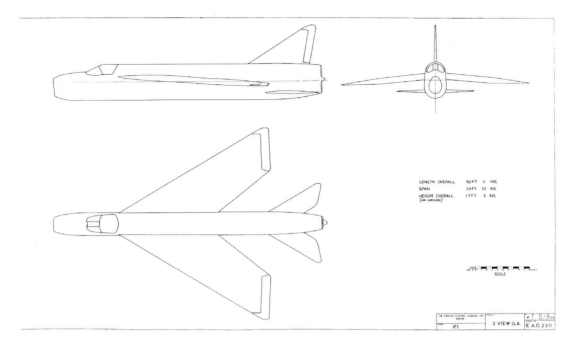

Layout for P1A as shown in Brochure 12, June 18, 1952.

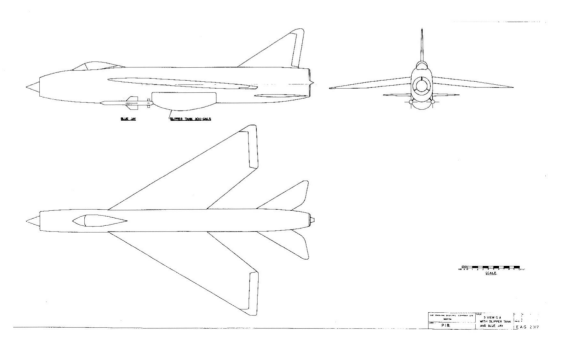

**The initial layout for P1B plus Blue Jay armament and 350 gallon
slipper tank for extra fuel, Brochure 12, June 18, 1952.**

Artist's impression of P1B, Brochure 12, June 18, 1952.

arise out of the opinions expressed by yourself and DOR in various discussions. I am however anxious that the weight should not get out of hand and spoil the altitude performance. I do think that this is a point which will have to be watched very carefully."

On the same day, also in a covering letter for copies of the brochure, Page wrote to DMARD: "These proposals are not based on any official MOS specification or Air Ministry operational requirement, but arise out of a meeting held at MOS under the chairmanship of DMARD on July 11, 1951. Furthermore, at a meeting held at MOS on June 9, 1952, a decision was taken to order additional F23/49 prototypes and it was suggested that these should have the modified nose fuselage. We have now received instructions to proceed with these additional prototypes and would therefore appreciate your comments on our proposals as soon as possible."

On July 28, Page asked the production organisation to commence the manufacture of three additional sets of parts similar to those of the second prototype except for the nose fuselage, pending the decision on the nose design. He stressed that this work should not delay the flight dates of the first and second prototypes.

Meanwhile, with the first prototype under construction to the original design, controversies remained to be resolved. The Short SB5 was nearing completion with the 50° wing and high-set tailplane. It flew for the first time on December 2. By this time, the P1A's 60° wing was already under construction. The SB5 would fly with the 60° wing, but still with the high tailplane, on July 29, 1953; by which time P1A construction was well advanced. The SB5 would not fly in the P1 configuration (60° wing and low tailplane) until January 1954 when the P1A was almost complete.

The results of the test flights showed that the English Electric wind tunnel analysis was correct and the P1 configuration offered superior handling characteristics. By this time, it had already been accepted that the main useful role of the SB5 in the P1 programme would be to allow English Electric

test pilot Roland Beamont to familiarise himself with the flight characteristics of the highly swept wing. Although the testing did not show any need to change the basic P1 configuration; it did betray a slight lateral 'twitchiness' at low speed. Subsequent wind tunnel tests clarified the problem and a search of NACA reports indicated that a small notch in the leading edge of the P1 wing would solve the problem by stabilising the flow at high incidence.

Work had continued to refine the P1B design. By early 1953, the firm believed that design development had reached a stage that offered considerably better operational capabilities than first envisaged. Furthermore, the Deputy Controller of Supplies (Air), Walter Puckey, had asked if the firm "were taking into account all the latest experience and knowledge that was being gained at the expense of a great deal of trouble on the present new high-speed fighters". This led to an exchange between Freddie Page and the Deputy Director of the RAE, John Serby, which raised a wide range of topics to be examined in the context of the latest P1 design. As a basis for such discussions, on February 5, 1953, only two months after the first flight of the SB5, EECo issued the new brochure describing the latest design.

This gave a detailed description of P1A and P1B with performance estimates supported by evidence from 69 research reports. The general arrangement of the P1B was little changed apart from a revision of the canopy, the addition of a dorsal spine to house some system items and a revised slipper tank of 250 gals for subsonic flight only. One of the items eventually fitted in the spine was an isopropyl nitrate starter which allowed autonomous starting when away from base. The firm accepted this with great reluctance since it had already caused fires in Javelins and had various reliability problems.

The main changes were internal to the nose. The four-gun installation had two in the upper nose and two in the lower nose. Alternative fits replaced the lower guns with either two Blue Jay missiles or drop-down packs containing 62 2in rockets. The radar in all cases was Radar Ranging Mk 2. It was noted,

Left: Bottom wing spar booms in jigs, March 26, 1952. Centre: Port wing spar in jig, July 17, 1952. Right: Wing spars and ribs in jig, February 4, 1953. While the Short SB5 was being built so that the Ministry of Supply could decide the best wing sweep angle for the P1, English Electric was already building the 60° wing for the P1 prototype, as shown in this sequence of photographs.

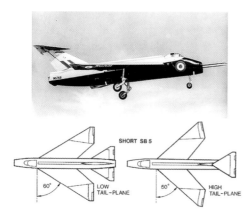

The Short SB5 made its first flight on December 2, 1952, with 50° wing sweep. It would not fly with 60° wing sweep until July 29, 1953, and not with the low tailplane until January 1954.

however, that the 28in diameter centre-body could accommodate a larger search and track radar giving the potential for all-weather operation.

ENGLISH ELECTRIC P6

All the P1A and B prototypes were to be powered by the Sapphire Sa5 model. The predicted maximum speed was a little over Mach 1.6. In a final section of the brochure entitled 'Further Developments', it was noted that EECo was going to offer a version of F23/49 with Sa7 engines as one of its tender submissions against the research specification ER134T. This had a new project number, P6. It would have greatly

increased performance, potentially well beyond M1.7 to M2.0 or more. Furthermore, the increased fuselage volume to fit the new engines would also allow a fuselage-mounted undercarriage and hence more fuel volume and better weapon carriage. The potential value of this route was stressed in covering letters to DMARD and ACAS(OR).

This brochure was still responding to the original specification from three years earlier. Now, on February 25, a first draft of the second issue was published based on OR268 incorporating Amendment 1 and with an attached draft Standard of Preparation for the third and subsequent prototypes. It was dispatched to English Electric on March 16. The specification incorporated the new nose design. The operational requirement was unchanged, calling for a day fighter with two or more guns and ranging radar and the longer term possibility of rocket armament. The Standard of Preparation, however, reflected the armament proposed in the brochure, calling for two or four Blue Jays plus two guns or 60 air-to-air rockets plus two guns or four guns. Mark 2 Ranging Radar was only required as an interim fit until a simple single-seat search radar became available.

The most recent discussion on equipment had been during a visit to Warton by Air Commodores Kyle and Evans, DOR(A) and (B), on February 18. They had resurrected the idea of fitting the Hughes E4 radar system. It was said that the North American

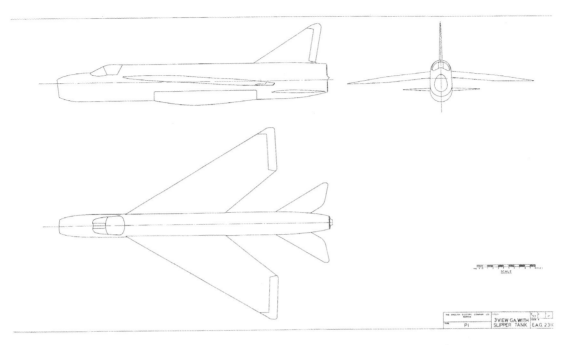

Drawing EAG 2310 showing P1A with a proposed slipper tank in Brochure 14, February 5, 1953.

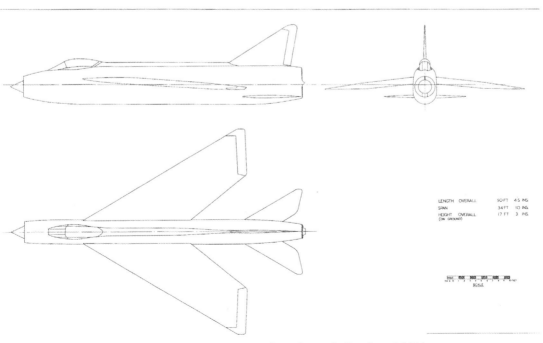

Drawing EAG 2308 showing a revised P1B layout in Brochure 14, February 5, 1953. Note the addition of the spine behind the cockpit canopy.

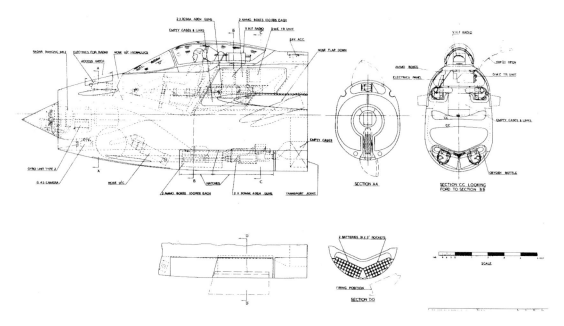

Drawing EAG 2313 showing the revised cockpit and nose layout for P1B including a changed four-gun arrangement. Brochure 14, February 5, 1953.

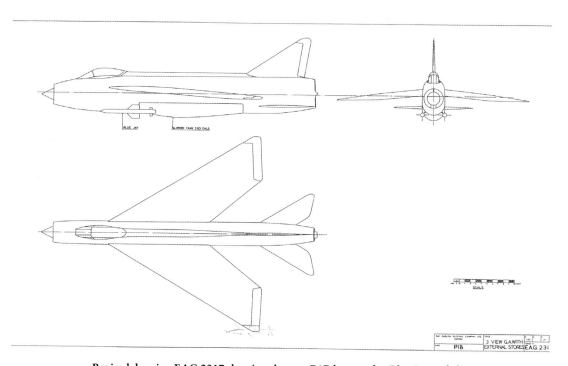

Revised drawing EAG 2317 showing the new P1B layout plus Blue Jay and the revised, slimmer, 250 gallon slipper tank, Brochure 14, February 5, 1953.

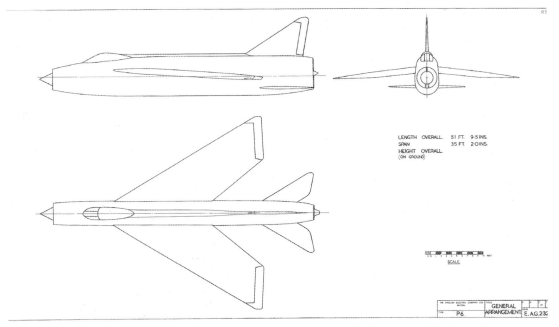

LENGTH OVERALL. 51 FT. 9·5 INS.
SPAN 35 FT. 2·0 INS.
HEIGHT OVERALL.
(ON GROUND)

SCALE

THE ENGLISH ELECTRIC COMPANY LTD. TITLE
WARTON GENERAL
ARRANGEMENT E.AG.232
TYPE P6.

**Drawing EAG 2323 showing the general arrangement of P6 with the increased fuselage volume
to accommodate Sapphire Sa7 engines. Offered as a research aircraft to Specification ER134T,
it was suggested as a better basis for a fighter than P1, Brochure 14, February 5, 1953.**

F-86D achieved 20 miles detection with a 22in dish
and that F23/49 should have at least 10 miles detection range. It was a desirable aim to design one type
of fighter capable of both all-weather operation and
day interception. They suggested armament for
P1B of two guns plus Blue Jay and the Hughes E4
search radar or Mark 2 Ranging Radar. Alternatively,
the Blue Jay could be replaced by two more guns
or a rocket battery in that order. As to the possible
Mach 2 fighter variant of P6 with Sa7 engines, they
suggested an armament of Blue Jay (minimum of
four) or Red Dean and two 30mm guns plus some
form of pilot-operated AI equipment.

An ADC was called for April 7 to finalise Issue 2
of F23/49. In preparation, the specialists at EECo
prepared comprehensive notes pointing out the
inconsistencies between the draft documents, the
challenges posed by the multiplicity of equipment
items and noting the areas where the current design
struggled to meet the requirements. Among other
things, they stressed the high supersonic drag of some

of the radio aerials and queried the apparent unnecessary duplication between some items.

For its part, the RAE produced a detailed commentary on the latest brochure. This was generally favourable, but listed detailed reservations in a number of
areas particularly with reference to stability and
control, design of the powered control system, a
few equipment items and the armour protection
proposed. In a covering letter, the Deputy Director described areas where the RAE might be able
to give advice and recommended the approaches to
be adopted in areas requiring further investigation.
Page replied with thanks, adding two other topics of
interest and looking forward to a joint review meeting
on the day after the ADC.

The ADC was held on April 7, attended by five
representatives from English Electric and 29 from
the Air Ministry, Ministry of Supply and RAE. It
addressed in detail the Standard of Preparation then
the Operational Requirement and finally the Specification. Various changes were agreed or, where

wording was left unchanged, possible difficulties were recognised and accepted. Page's criticism of the radar requirement as out of date and his plea for progress with a single-seat search radar was accepted. With regard to performance, it was accepted that the requirement would apply to the clean aircraft until such time as the effect of Blue Jay carriage and the slipper tank were better understood.

AN OPERATIONAL AIRCRAFT

It was now about five years since the start of the project. The Air Force, however, was still concerned that MoS ambitions for the P1 as a research aircraft might disrupt the development of the fighter. In early 1951, ACAS(OR) Air Vice Marshal Claude Pelly had written to DGTD(A) Stewart Scott-Hall emphasising that F23/49 was a 'development' programme for an operational aircraft and not a 'research' programme. Nevertheless, MoS technical oversight had continued to put a strong emphasis on the research element.

Now, on April 10, 1953, ACAS(OR) Air Vice Marshal Geoffrey Tuttle wrote to PDSR(A) Ernest Jones expressing his concern about attitudes within the MoS towards F23/49 as a research programme. He attached a detailed history of the RAF's leading role in the programme. In reply, Jones assured him that the MoS was not trying to run it as a research item, but he pressed the case for the RAE to take the lead in testing the aircraft.

He urged that, given Beamont's inexperience, the aircraft should be handed over to the expert pilots at the RAE as soon as possible for them to conduct the testing. Tuttle in response pointed out, "You will know that the ace of aces on delta aircraft from RAE was sent down to fly the Javelin. He was such an expert that he crashed it." He suggested that any flying by the RAE should be done at Boscombe Down. This ended the exchange, but the controversy lingered on. The design work, however, now focused on the operational aspects of the aircraft.

Over the next five years, the official requirement and specification were subject to steady evolution and expansion. These changes were in response to changing military perspectives and increasing technical capabilities. Choices and progress continued to be affected by the goals for other projects.

The second issue of F23/49 finally emerged on June 3, 1953. The accompanying Appendix B was still OR268 plus Amendment List 1 but with a note acknowledging that changes agreed at the ADC had not yet been incorporated. The specification itself introduced the fundamental change to both day and night operation, but EECo was disconcerted to find that many of the detailed changes agreed at the ADC had not been incorporated.

During the same month, OR268 draft Issue 3 began Ministry circulation. (There had never been a formal Issue 2. The number 3 was a typing error but was retained for the formal issue to avoid further confusion.) Also, on June 19, the firm was sent a draft issue of OR318 for an Advanced Jet Trainer with the request to examine the possibility of meeting the requirement by modifying a fighter of the same generation. Meanwhile, over the same period, the ongoing work on P6 to ER134T aroused Tuttle's interest in Mach 2 fighter possibilities or an F23/49 option with a single Gyron or RB106 engine and fuselage-mounted undercarriage.

CHANGING TO ROLLS-ROYCE

After completing the P6 studies, in September 1953 attention turned to the response to OR318 with twin-seat variants of P1B with either Sa5 or RA24 engines. The latter were already the subject of a proposal being developed for P1B to overcome the endurance deficiency of the Sapphire-engined design. Also, compared to the Sa7 option examined for P6, the RA24 gave a similar dramatic increase in speed without needing major structural changes. A brochure for the F23/49 trainer variant was produced in October with RA24 as the chosen engine.

The change to the RA24 for P1B had already been agreed by the Air Staff and DMARD(RAF) Air Commodore Glynn Silyn Roberts had requested go-ahead agreement from DGTD(A) George Gardner. In November, the company produced a brochure

STEADY LEVEL MANOEUVRE BOUNDARIES

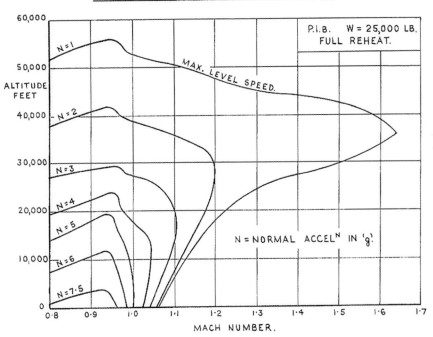

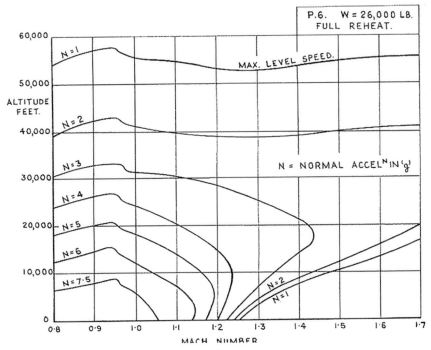

These graphs show the much larger flight envelope and higher speeds offered
by P6 compared to P1, Brochure 14, February 5, 1953.

in response to F23/49 Issue 2 based on P1B with RA24 engines. With these engines, the flight envelope was extended in speed and altitude far beyond that of the Sa5 powered version in the February brochure. The ceiling was raised to 60,000ft and the speed would potentially reach far beyond Mach 2. It was, however, realistically placarded at a maximum of Mach 2.

Ideally, operation beyond Mach 1.7 was thought to require a variable intake but EECo believed that operation up to Mach 2 might be possible with careful throttle handling. The brochure data was for a fixed intake. Armstrong Siddeley tried to promote its P163 development of the Sapphire as an alternative to the RA24; but EECo pointed out that this was still in the design stage whereas the RA24 was aleady running.

DEVELOPMENT BATCH

At the end of November, Issue 3 of OR268 was published. The rationale for the new issue was that technical developments since the first issue allowed more ambitious operational objectives. It dropped the preamble about ground-controlled visual interception (GCI) — the role was to intercept bombers flying at speeds up to Mach 1 and heights up to 50,000ft and above by day or night as soon as possible after detection by the early warning system. It was to be primarily a Blue Jay carrier and would be fitted with a search radar to OR3563 or Radar Ranging Mk.3 as an interim if necessary. The radar would be complemented by a wide-band homer, a VHF homer and new display and communication equipment, all covered by their own ORs. Entry into service was to be by 1957.

By this time the Operational Requirement and Standard of Preparation documents were all being framed to cover not only the two batches of prototypes (two P1A and three P1B) but also 20 'pre-production' or 'development' aircraft in two batches of 10.

There had been conflicting views about the challenge of meeting the 1957 in-service date. A year earlier, on January 2, 1953, AD/TD Plans, W H Curtis, had written to PDRD(A) Woodward-Nutt, DGTD(A) Scott-Hall and DMARD(RAF) Silyn Roberts, advocating an order for 20 pre-production aircraft to a

'relaxed standard' — to be followed, after a gap of 15 months, by production of the requisite number of aircraft to the full all-weather standard. This assumed that production quantities of AI 20 would be available by mid-1958 and that it proved practicable to fit AI 20 without radical redesign.

Curtis acknowledged that DGAP, W R McGaw, did not like the idea of pre-production aircraft or a gap in production. Both he and EECo would prefer continuous production, starting with an initial batch of 120 'relaxed standard' aircraft (approximating to a day fighter), 20 for CA and 100 for RAF service, followed smoothly by the production run of the full all-weather standard aircraft. Curtis went on to discuss a possible compromise option plus the possible benefit of introducing work towards a trainer version for which there was as yet no official requirement. Finally, he laid out details of the decisions needed urgently, especially with the prospect of considerable under-employment in 1955-56 due to the early run-down of Canberra work.

The introduction of the development batch was a radical departure from previous procurement practice. It was agreed by the Air Ministry and Ministry of Supply in late 1953 as a way of tackling the system complexities resulting from the new more ambitious design goals. On February 10, 1954, Victor Raby, Assistant Under-Secretary at the Air Ministry, wrote to Peter Humphreys-Davies, Under-Secretary at the Treasury, to request financing for the development batch. He explained at length the military requirement and technical objectives for a supersonic fighter equipped with an AI radar and armed with guided weapons.

Since this would mark a large step forward in capability, it was recommended that there should be extensive RAF flying to iron out operational problems in addition to the technical flight testing. Rather than have more hand-built prototypes, they proposed that a pre-production batch, built with limited jigs and tooling would be an economical way of shortening the development cycle before the start of full production.

He ended by requesting urgent authority to place an order for 20 pre-production aircraft at a total estimated

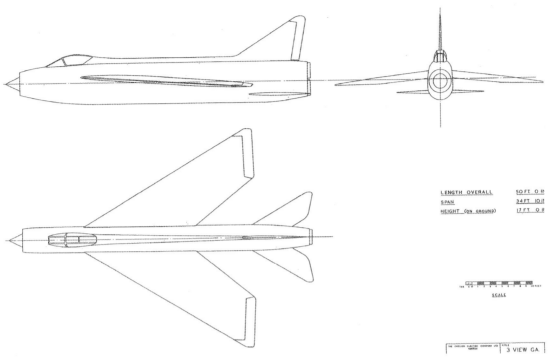

LENGTH OVERALL	50 FT. 0 IN
SPAN	34 FT. 10 IN
HEIGHT (ON GROUND)	17 FT. 0 IN

Drawing EAG 2353 showing P1B now with Rolls-Royce RA24 engines instead of Armstrong Siddeley Sapphire Sa5 engines, Brochure 19, November 9, 1953.

cost of £3.8m and to initiate step-by-step provision of production measures for aircraft and engines for 100 production aircraft at an estimated cost of £2m. Humphreys-Davies circulated this in the Treasury for comment. On the assumption that the Air Ministry reference to AI radar inevitably referred to AI 18, the question was raised as to the relationship between F23 and the Thin-wing Javelin programmes. A meeting was held with the MoS and Air Ministry on February 18 to clarify the situation.

On February 23, Humphreys-Davies wrote to Raby summarising the outcome, including: "We accepted the need to get this revolutionary aircraft into service as soon as possible. It could be regarded as the successor to Hunters and Swifts. It was explained that this did not affect the case for developing the Thin-wing Javelin, since the F23, while intended ultimately to be capable of night interception (with AI 20), could not fill the role of all-weather fighter, for 'frontal assault' on fast bombers under all conditions. This is mainly because it could not carry all the equipment required for this role, without unacceptable loss of speed."

At the same time, the Treasury accepted that the F23 was a sound aircraft but that the novel technical and operational problems it would present justified the "pre-production philosophy". The need for at least 20 aircraft was accepted in the light of the numbers required by various organisations for different purposes. The cost was likely to be £250,000 per aircraft according to the MoS rather than the £190,000 suggested by the Air Ministry. The funding would be split across MoS and Air Ministry budgets. On the question of releasing funding to start the main production investment, they accepted the Treasury request to defer this pending the development batch experience. The Air Ministry stressed, however, that there should be no unavoidable gap between pre-production and production proper such that it would "have to take production aircraft which could be used only as day fighters".

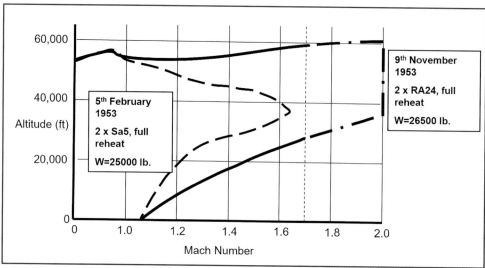

**This graph shows the large expansion of the flight envelope achieved
by the change to Rolls-Royce RA24 engines.**

Also on February 23, Humphreys-Davies forwarded the development batch proposal to Sir James Crombie, Treasury Third Secretary. He explained the case made by the MoS and Air Ministry and gave a brief outline of the rationale, emphasising the expected cost and timescale benefits, adding as background: "The Departments, sensitive to the criticism made against the time lag between first prototype and squadron service, propose to try and cut down the time spent in flight testing after the prototype stage. In the case of Swift and Hunter for instance, much valuable time has been lost (and probably a good deal of money, if it could be identified) through the aircraft being put into production merely on the results of the prototype tests and before finding out whether the machine is really suitable without further modification for operational service."

He pointed out that, although the pre-production aircraft would be more expensive than the production models, savings might be made overall by avoiding last-minute modifications on the production line. Crombie gave the go-ahead on February 25, writing on Humphreys-Davies' memo: "I agree that this is a proposal which we should accept. The additional

value which we shall get out of the aircraft as a result of earlier availability for operational use justifies the additional cost of the pre-production plan".

There were concerns in the Air Ministry and industry about the difficulty of ensuring efficient management of the development batch. On January 28, 1954, DOR(A) Kyle had a long discussion with Page about the Standard of Preparation for the F23 and the need to ensure that the 20 aircraft to be ordered would be produced in the least possible time and with the least possible interference from the various technical people of the MoS. They discussed an early ADC and the idea of producing Standards for the first and tenth aircraft as well as the 20th; otherwise, a large number of MoS specialists would work just to the existing OR and constantly interfere and impede progress. On February 20, Kyle asked DDOR1 to consider and discuss these ideas, writing "I was very impressed with Page's arguments about the MoS low level staff, and I do think we need to give guidance to them and, indirectly, help to the firm in this way".

The introduction of the development batch influenced the framing of all the future issues of the Operational Requirement and Specification.

Chapter 4

WEAPON SYSTEM DEVELOPMENT

Even before the formal publication of OR268 Issue 3, EECo started to feed back comments to the Air Ministry and MoS. At a meeting with DMARD Woodward-Nutt on November 23, 1954, Freddie Page pointed out that although there was much talk of the Ferranti radar and gun sight development; no prototype contracts had been received and this was seriously limiting the effort on the job. In the months following the formal publication of Issue 3, extensive scrutiny by EECo continued.

The firm provided detailed comments on the weight, space and performance implications of the requirements particularly in respect to the new items. It also queried the timescale for the availability of some equipment. An ADC was planned for February, but the number of topics raised concerning the OR led to a separate dedicated meeting on February 23, 1954. After this the firm produced a suggested revision of the OR. Following due consideration, Issue 4 of OR268 was sent out as a draft in March and issued on April 6.

The new OR formed Appendix B of the 3rd Issue of Specification F23/49 which was circulated on May 4. This then became the subject of an ADC held on June 1 with DMARD(RAF) Silyn Roberts in the chair. The chairman proposed that the specification should apply to the 20th aircraft of the development batch, but hoped that earlier aircraft would also meet this standard. Many items from the requirement and specification were discussed as regards challenges and uncertainties and proposed solutions.

As well as dealing with the details, EECo raised once again the general problem of the growing equipment load. They pointed out that they only controlled half of the final all-up weight of the aircraft, and that they must put certain provisos on their stated performance data. These included tolerances on drag and engine power plus reservations due to the unsettled status of Blue Jay and the embodiment loan equipment that was out of their control.

The firm had completed a study which showed how critically dependent performance was on size, weight and drag of ancillaries. At the Ministry's request it was agreed that this report should be distributed to equipment firms so that they could better appreciate the difficulties.

WEAPONS SYSTEM CONCEPT

EECo pleaded for closer co-operation with the equipment firms. Silyn Roberts expressed the greatest sympathy with this and said that it was now Ministry policy that an aircraft, its equipment and armament should be considered as a weapon system and that no decisions on the equipment and armament which might affect the airframe should be made without consulting the airframe designer. This new focus on the 'weapon system' concept would be a significant factor from now on.

As regards radar, it was agreed to drop Radar Ranging Mk 3 and instead to have AI 20 as the interim fit until AI 23 became available. OR268 was to be amended accordingly.

A revised draft of F23/49 Issue 3 was circulated on July 7 for comments prior to signing off by DMARD(RAF) the next week. It was issued on August 10.

Recent experience in developing a Canberra variant capable of operating at up to 60,000ft led EECo to examine P1 developments to intercept such targets. The method finally selected was to fit a pair of rocket motors in a detachable pack shaped like the ventral tank and fully interchangeable with it. The study results were reported in a brochure on June 17. These showed that the interception ceiling could be raised to 60,000ft or higher by employing a zoom manoeuvre to reach that altitude and then using the thrust of a single rocket motor to sustain that altitude for the engagement. The second motor would be used when necessary to aid manoeuvring.

The P1A made its first flight on August 4, 1954. Although not fitted with reheat, it went supersonic on August 11. The aircraft would prove to have none of the handling problems forecast by the RAE. In February 1958, a report to the Defence Research Policy Committee would state: "This aircraft has to date been particularly free of major aerodynamic and structural problems, in particular none of the vices such as pitch-up, which have afflicted the majority of recent fighter projects, including most of the American supersonic aircraft, have been encountered on the P1." And in January 1959, DDOR4 Group Captain Andrew Humphrey, would write, "During the past year the flying characteristics of the Lightning have been shown to be good throughout, and even beyond, its specified performance envelope."

The mixed power-plant concept was incorporated into a comprehensive response to Issue 3 of Specification F23/49 in a brochure dated November 5, 1954. The bulk of the brochure described P1B, but a brief initial review of P1A mentioned that drag measurements were in hand as part of the flight trials. When complete, they would be used to update the brochure performance estimates.

Externally, the P1B was basically as shown in previous brochures but with the definitive jettisonable ventral tank and exchangeable rocket motor pack as per the June brochure. The maximum speed envelope was still shown up to Mach 2—implying a potential Mach 2+ capability. Most changes were internal. It introduced the idea of exchangeable weapon packs in the lower nose fuselage. The radar was to be AI 23 or the interim AI 20, but as yet there were no installation details.

While these P1 developments were under way, throughout 1954, a working party chaired by Sir Arnold Hall studied the future of air defence in all its aspects on behalf of the Air Council. Their conclusions with regard to fighters were to guide the specification of the new fighter to requirement OR329 which was issued in the same month as the start of the working party. In the final report, the RAE specialists recommended fighter designs with long slender fuselages, straight wings, podded engines and high tailplanes. They bore a strong resemblance to the Bristol Type 188—which the RAE had chosen as meeting the ER134 research aircraft specification. A Lightning-like configuration was presented as an unsatisfactory alternative. Specification F155T was issued in early 1955 at about the time of the final report.

Even before F155T was circulated, OR329 was affecting thinking about all the other fighter programmes. An example is found in a paper by OR16 on October

19, 1954, making the case for continued investment in the Rocket Fighter. This looked at the period 1956 to 1964 and predicted that the Soviet Type 37 and 39 jet bombers could increase their attack altitude to about 47,000ft by operating at light fuel loads on short range missions. With engine development and reduced armament, they could increase this to over 50,000ft by 1960. From 1962 onwards, there could be a Mach 1.3 bomber operating at 60,000ft. It further predicted that, until the arrival of the OR329 fighter in 1962, most of the planned fighters (Hunter, Swift, Javelin, 545, F23, Thin-wing Javelin) would be unable to cope with this growing threat due to their inadequate realistic intercept ceiling (taken to be the 1.5g ceiling).

Only the Rocket Fighter offered the necessary much higher ceiling. The day fighter prototypes from Avro and Saunders-Roe (to F137 and F138 against OR301) or a possible new AI-equipped type with a larger jet engine (to F177 against OR337) would fill the gap between 1959 and 1962. They would also give the RAF experience of operating rocket fighters ahead of the arrival of the OR329 which, it was assumed, would be a mixed power-plant fighter. In spite of the fact that only a small number of rocket fighters was required, there was no consideration of the rocket-boosting of P1B in the F23 figures quoted. OR268 Issue 5 was published on February 24, 1955.

RADAR

During the period 1954-56, three key items were central to the weapon system development: the radar, the armament and the design of the cockpit displays for single-seat all-weather operation. As to the radar, EECo began discussions with Ferranti about AI 23 in February 1954. At about the same time, however, the Radar Research Establishment (RRE) began promoting AI 20. At the review of Issue 3 of OR268 on February 23, 1954, there was still great official uncertainty about the radar options and their timescales for availability.

Industry continued to be concerned about the cost and timescale burden of having to design for three different radar options. On March 29, EECo wrote to MoS "…we should like your assurance that Ranging Radar Mk.3 will be the subject of early contract action to ensure availability for the F23/49, and that it will be available sufficiently far in advance of the AI 20 spiral scan system to make it worthwhile with regard to the extra design work involved in providing alternative installations. We are also concerned about similar considerations in relation to IFF 10 with SIF versus new FIS system." The response on April 23, in a letter covering Issue 4 of OR268, said, "As regards our discussion on Radar Ranging Mk.3, although there is a firm intention to develop the equipment, the application policy is by no means clear yet and I am doing what I can to get the matter resolved." However, after the selection of AI 20 at the ADC on June 1 in preference to Radar Ranging Mk 3 and the issue of OR3572 on July 5, the installation design focused on AI 23 and AI 20.

EECo were initially enthusiastic about AI 20 for its smallness and simplicity in spite of an unimpressive demonstration flight at Defford on April 8. As time went on, however, installation problems emerged. AI 23 was being designed specifically in response to OR3563 aimed at the P1B's needs, whereas AI 20 was an RRE experimental system that was now being productionised against OR3572. These different pedigrees impacted the installation design task.

Thus we find Page writing to Gardner, Director General Technical Development (Air), on May 20, 1954: "Whilst these arrangements have gone ahead satisfactorily with Messrs Ferranti, it is apparently the intention of RRE to develop their equipment on the old-fashioned lines." The problem was that while Ferranti was making every effort to match AI 23 to the Lightning intake nose cone, both RRE and E K Cole were loath to adapt AI 20 accordingly in case it compromised its installation in other aircraft including the Vickers N113 (Scimitar) and Type 545 Developed Swift. Hence, although both radars continued to be assessed throughout 1955 and 1956; installation work at EECo focused increasingly on AI 23.

Anything that might affect the timescale for

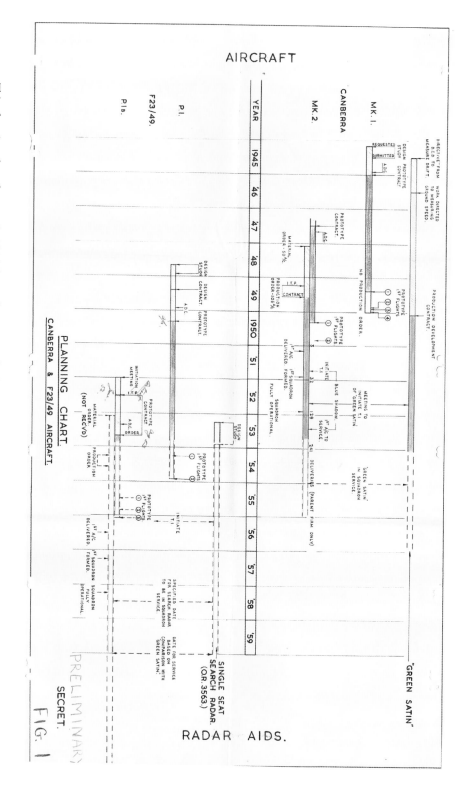

This planning chart from early 1954 shows the projected schedule for integrating AI 23 (OR3563) into P1B in the context of the overall P1 programme and in comparison with the experience of integrating Green Satin into Canberra Mark 2.

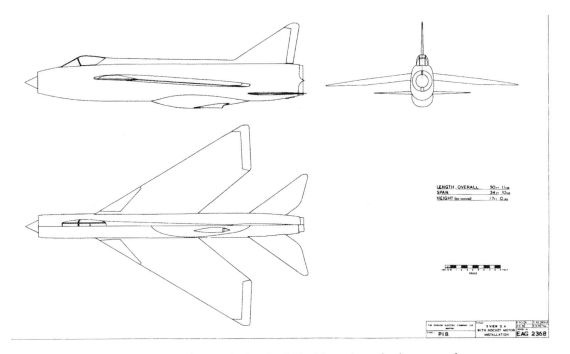

Drawing EAG 2368 Issue A, showingP1B with a twin-rocket booster pack replacing the slipper tank, Brochure 23, June 17, 1954.

A single rocket unit under test, Brochure 23, June 17, 1954.

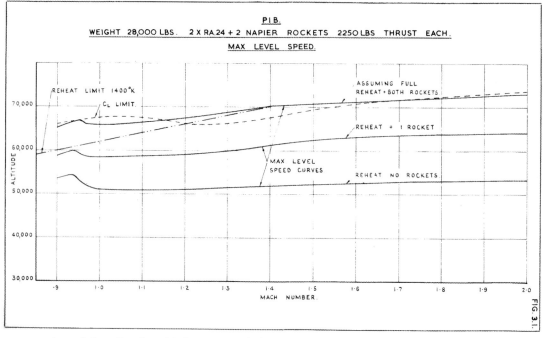

A graph from Brochure 23, June 17, 1954, showing the P1B maximum altitude versus speed for three cases: maximum reheat, reheat plus one rocket and maximum reheat plus two rockets. At supersonic speeds, each rocket raises the ceiling by 8000 to 10,000ft.

developing the two radars caused concern. For instance, at the fourth progress meeting for AI 23 on January 31, 1956, Ferranti complained that CVD contracts on English Electric Valve Co and Mullard to develop magnetrons had no priority. The items offered so far did not meet the Ferranti specification and thus there might be no suitable valve available for the pre-production programme. RRE replied that, as there was a proposal to use AI 20 (which also used these magnetrons) for another role as well as AI, it might be possible to obtain higher priority on the strength of this application.

EECo was concerned that AI 23 might be delayed for F23/49 by work to adapt it for other aircraft. Ferranti offered assurances that Saunders-Roe had agreed to fit it unchanged to the P177. Similarly, on March 14, the company was told that de Havilland, considering it as an alternative to AI 18 for the DH110, was happy to take it unchanged.

Throughout 1955 and 1956 there was rising concern

about increased costs. In July 1955, the MoS informed the Treasury that, in addition to the £5m agreed for the production of 20 development batch aircraft, it had now realised that this involved a considerable amount of design work, model, rig and structural testing, general development and flight testing that would cost a further £1.5m.

Then, in November 1955, the Air Ministry pressed for commitment to early production of AI 20 to ensure that initial production aircraft would not lack pilot-operated AI radars. In December it pressed for an order for 60 crash production models of AI 20 for the F23 at a cost of £400,000. Although the Treasury was not convinced of the case; it finally agreed in February 1956 but expressed grave doubts as to whether the crash programme was essential since the aircraft programme might slip. Furthermore, the short service life of AI 20 pending the availability of AI 23 was an additional objection to unnecessary expenditure. Industry shared these concerns.

P1A first prototype WG760 takes off on its first flight.

On February 3, 1956, Page wrote to Ferranti committing EECo to do whatever was necessary to ensure the timely delivery of AI 23 and PAS (Pilot's Attack Sight). He also expressed concern that MoS was still quoting a 1961 delivery date for AI 23 although the programme was running well ahead of this. Moreover, the official 1961 date meant that EECo was being forced to consider more AI 20 installations than it felt was justified. He finished by detailing all the actions being taken to overcome problems that had arisen with regard to materials and bought out items for the radar installation.

In July 1956 the MoS met with EECo to discuss the whole problem of cost estimation. The estimate for the P1B prototypes had risen from £1,227,663 in March 1954 to £2,836,970 in March 1956. The MoS proposed that no design changes should be undertaken until an estimate had been made of the cost implications. EECo pointed out that it was necessary to do the design work to understand the cost implications. Furthermore, it was noted that, although the requirements of Specification Issue 4 were now known; the contract was still against Specification Issue 2 and that was still theoretically the basis for budgeting. Nevertheless, the company agreed that some of the alterations and changes could have been visualised financially in March 1954 and that the estimates had been to some extent undervalued.

There was discussion as to the difficulty of estimating flight test costs and the recently introduced maintenance requirements. In addition, the increased jig and tool costs resultant from the design changes were discussed and so too was the fact that rising wage rates and overheads were elements outside the company's control. The meeting closed with the MoS representatives agreeing that they had gained a very useful appreciation of the problems surrounding estimates for prototypes of advanced designs of aircraft and that the approach to estimating showed a considerable improvement since 1954. They would write back with proposals for improving the methods of dealing with financial conditions in prototype and development contracts.

MISSILE CONFUSION

As well as the inherent installation design problems, further potential radar complications were raised by the air-to-air missile programme. Although Blue Jay was the specified armament, other missiles continued to be considered. On August 7, 1954, EECo was informed that the Air Staff, with the agreement of the MoS, had proposed the development of a new high-altitude version of Blue Sky for carriage by F23. Studies were now under way at Fairey, Ferranti and RRE. EECo co-operation was requested.

Page agreed but with a plea that this activity should in no way delay the radar programme. A meeting on September 17 revealed that the missile would be

P1A WG760 in flight.

a completely new vehicle and that three guidance options were being considered. These were beam-riding, command guidance or semi-active homing. While the missile could be carried in the same way as Blue Jay, all the guidance options presented problems, with semi-active possibly being the least disruptive. On December 9, EECo was informed that High Altitude Blue Sky had been cancelled.

On May 22, 1956, Mallison 'Mal' Powley of Ferranti wrote to Page warning him that Sir Stewart Mitchell (Controller Guided Weapons and Electronics) had recently enquired about the possibility of adding CW injection to AI 23. This was to support the use of Sparrow Mk 3 by the P177 (SR177) aircraft in order to overcome the weather limitations of Blue Jay. Obviously, the same rationale might apply to the P1 with severe repercussions due to the major increase in space and cooling requirements.

These were minor distractions and detailed design including installation mock-ups for Blue Jay proceeded through 1955 and 1956. Questions soon arose however as to exactly which variant of Blue Jay should be the focus of attention. Towards the end of 1954, there was finally sufficient detail available about Blue Jay to begin assessment of its impact on aircraft performance, to begin detailed design of its installation and to develop the missile aiming and firing system. Its seeker's narrow beamwidth and search pattern (out to $3\frac{1}{2}°$ off-boresight) required accurate aiming.

There was uncertainty as to whether to align the missile with the airstream for minimum drag or with the guns for aiming. Also, what extra provision was needed in the gunsight to allow for the fact that missile aiming did not need allowance for gravity drop? If a firing was to be successful, the target needed to be between the missile's maximum and minimum firing ranges. Range information could be provided by any of the radars under consideration. AI 23, however, had a lock-follow facility so that it could also be used to point the missile seeker at the target to improve target acquisition.

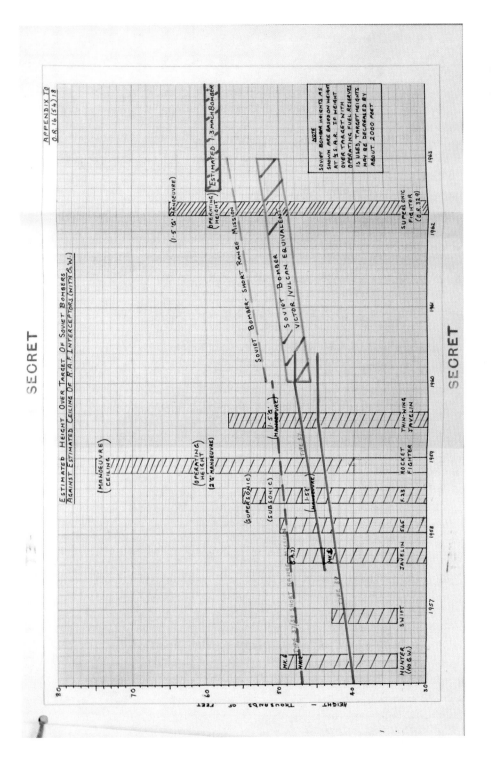

Graph from OR16 paper making the case for the Rocket Fighter, October 19, 1954. It shows the anticipated increase in altitude for bomber attacks over the period 1956-1964. In comparison, it shows the expected useful interception altitude bands for various planned fighter types at their year of entry into service. It suggests that, until the mixed power plant fighter to specification F155 (OR329) enters service, only the Rocket Fighter will have an adequate ceiling. (TNA AIR 20/8596)

As design work to incorporate these features began, EECo became aware that de Havilland Propellers was beginning to explore developments of Blue Jay such as bigger wings to allow interception at higher altitudes and a more sensitive seeker to allow target detection at wider aspect angles. As early as February 10, 1955, Powley was writing to EECo to report on a meeting at MoS concerning harmonization of the guns, gunsight and Blue Jay. He would note: "There was complete confusion at the meeting about which versions of Blue Jay would have the homing eye aligned with the missile body and which would have it trainable, and why." In the same letter he summarised Ferranti's proposals for AI 23 to provide seeker pointing up to 5° off-boresight for four Blue Jays.

From this point until 1958, there would be continuous debate over which Blue Jay variant should be the prime weapon for the Lightning. As things panned out, there were three versions under consideration: Blue Jay Mk1 (which would eventually go into service as Firestreak), Mk2 and Mk3. Also, EECo had been working on a Lightning-based interceptor to meet F155T. Through this work, the company was aware that there was a fourth version of Blue Jay under development, the Mk4, to meet part of OR1131 for air-to-air missiles for the F155.

To add to the confusion, this fourth version was being run by a separate branch within the MoS. While Blue Jay Marks 1, 2 and 3 were the managed on one of the branches that led via the Assistant Director of Guided Weapons (Air) to the Director of Guided Weapons Projects, Blue Jay Mk4 (under code name Blue Vesta) was managed on one of the branches that led via the Assistant Director of Guided Weapons (New Projects) to the Director of Guided Weapons R&D. In late November 1955, a note summarised EECo's understanding of the situation regarding infra-red weapons for P1B and P8. They believed that P1B would enter service in 1958, initially armed with Blue Jay Mk1, and P8 would enter service in 1961 armed with Blue Vesta. However, they had been given the following Blue Jay production proposal from de Havilland: Blue Jay Marks 1 and 2 were intended

to arm the DH110 (Sea Vixen), Hunter and Javelin. Blue Jay Mk 1, with a lead sulphide (PbS) seeker, would enter production in January 1957. Mark 2, with a new lead telluride (PbTe) seeker, would enter production in January 1958. Both marks would be capable of launch at speeds up to M0.95 and altitude up to 55,000ft. (It was later agreed that they could be launched from P1B at up to M1.5 above 34,000ft).

Blue Jay Mk3 was intended for P1B and the Saunders-Roe SR53 mixed-propulsion fighter. It would have the lead telluride seeker but also bigger wings and be capable of launch at M1.7 at 60,000ft altitude. It would go into production in June 1959. All of these variants would have a maximum seeker look angle of 30° and thus be tail-chase weapons (to be fired within 20° off the target's tail).

The F155's Blue Jay Mk4 would also have the lead telluride seeker and bigger wings, but would have a 60° look angle limit to allow full exploitation of the seeker in firings at much higher angles off the target's tail. It would enter production in January 1961 and be cleared for launch at up to M2.0 and 60,000ft.

Much of the data was provisional and the figures would only be firmed up over the next two years. EECo had already challenged them, particularly in regard to carriage and firing limitations. Two problems predominated. Firstly, the new variants had hemispherical nose windows instead of the pointed, faceted Mk1 nose. This made them more prone to aerodynamic heating. There were concerns that the P1B's higher speed would cause overheating during prolonged carriage or at the missile's peak boost speed after high-speed firings.

De Havilland even proposed a Blue Jay Mk2A with a de-rated motor to reduce the maximum speed. EECo believed that de Havilland was being too pessimistic by not making enough allowance for thermal lag in assessing the rate of heating or taking account of typical speeds in realistic interception missions. For instance, most tail-chase firings would be at well below maximum speed because of speed loss during the pursuit turn.

Secondly, the larger wings of Blue Jay Marks 3 and 4 allowed interception at higher altitudes but suffered

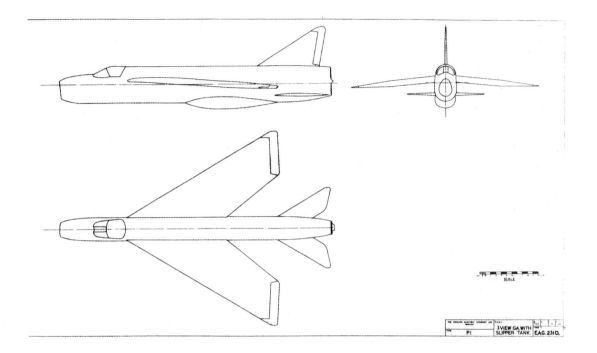

Revised drawing EAG 2310 showing P1A with the latest slipper tank, Brochure 26, November 5, 1954.

control power limitations below 15,000ft. Over the next three years, the evolving design of the missile, its integration and its operational use would be subject to extensive study and review before final agreement on the way ahead.

COCKPIT DISPLAYS

The first P1A, having made 50 flights, was handed over to A&AEE at Boscombe Down on March 9, 1955, for an initial appraisal. The second P1A (WG763) made its first flight on July 18, 1955. As well as continuing the performance and handling trials, it began weapons testing with gunfire trials in January 1956.

Draft Specification F23/49 Issue 4 dated February 24, 1956, incorporating OR268 Issue 5, was circulated to industry on March 23. It was intended to apply to the third, fourth and fifth prototypes and the 20 aircraft of the development batch. It was sent out for comment prior to issue in April, but the difficulties highlighted revealed developmental problems that delayed publication for a year.

In his initial eight-page response to the draft, Page commented on more than 40 items in the specification and the requirement. He pointed out the inconsistencies between the documents, especially in respect of performance goals. Many of the detailed comments noted that progress against the specification was stalled by lack of information about items of equipment—all of which were out of the firm's control.

Furthermore, some items would not be available in time to fit to any of the development aircraft. His general conclusion was that the continual revision of the specification and the slipping schedule of equipment availability meant that the value of the development batch was being lost.

The operational utility of the radar and weapons was entirely dependent on the successful integration of their displays and controls with the other cockpit instruments and equipment. Among these was a

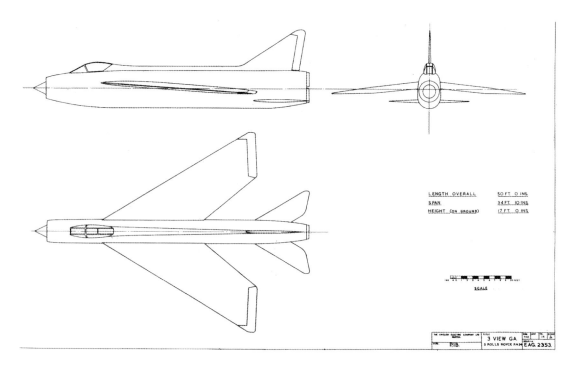

Drawing EAG 2353, P1B, Brochure 26, November 5, 1954.

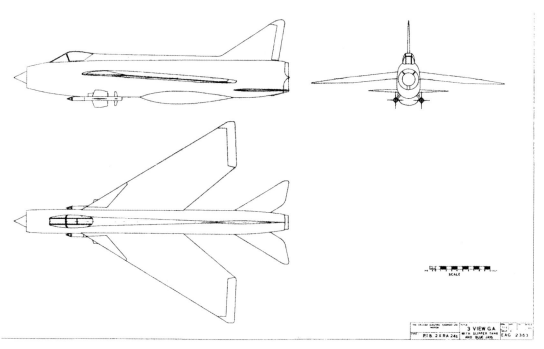

Drawing EAG 2363, P1B with Blue Jay and slipper tank, Brochure 26, November 5, 1954.

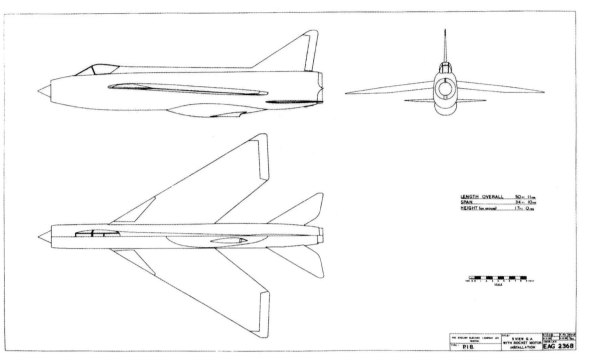

**Drawing EAG 2368 Issue B, again showing P1B with a twin-rocket
booster pack, Brochure 26, November 5, 1954.**

new suite of flight instruments to OR946, issued on July 16, 1954. This was required for all fighter aircraft with performance equal to or greater than F23/49 but was needed initially in time for F23. The RAE was the design authority. Detailed investigation for F23 only began in late 1955 and significant conflicts were revealed during 1956.

The interaction between the OR946 instrument suite and the Elliott auto-pilot needed rationalisation. In addition, space conflicts between OR946, the pilot's sight and leg-room were hard to resolve. It was eventually agreed that a test version of OR946 would be fitted to the 12th development aircraft, but the production standard would not be ready until after the first 40 to 50 production aircraft. It required a redesign of several of the aircraft's equipment bays and revised wiring.

These development problems led to the realisation that weapon systems could not be developed piecemeal. The weapon system concept had been introduced for F23 at the ADC in June 1954 and a detailed explanatory paper had been issued by OR16 in November 1955. Only now, however, was it acknowledged that an integrated weapon system's development needed managing in its totality. At a meeting on September 18, 1956, to review the second draft of Issue 4 of F23/49, it was noted that a new clause required the contractor to "be responsible for the effective integration of the aircraft and its equipment in order to provide the Services with the most effective weapon system meeting the operational requirements of this specification".

Freddie Page accepted, but expressed concern that it would be hampered by the firm still having no design control over the equipment to be integrated. Years later, in his memoirs, he would suggest that the development batch approach had been a mistake because the multiplicity of aircraft, all at different modification standards, actually inhibited the development of the integrated system. Trying to maintain

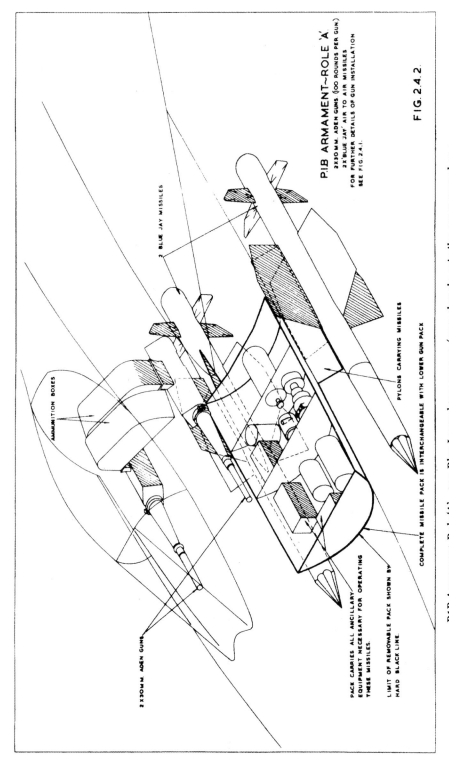

P1B Armament-Role 'A' – two Blue Jay and two cannon (note that the missiles are mounted on a removable pack to facilitate armament role changes), Brochure 26, November 5, 1954.

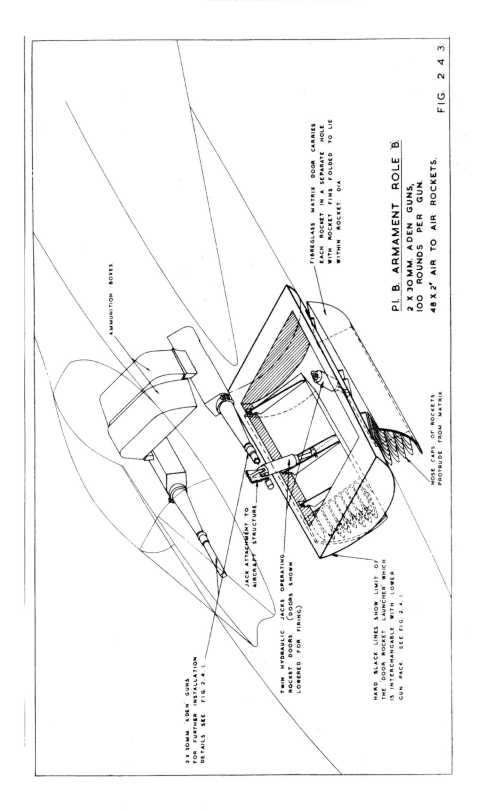

P1B Armament-Role 'B' – 48 x 2in air-to-air rockets and two cannon, Brochure 26, November 5, 1954.

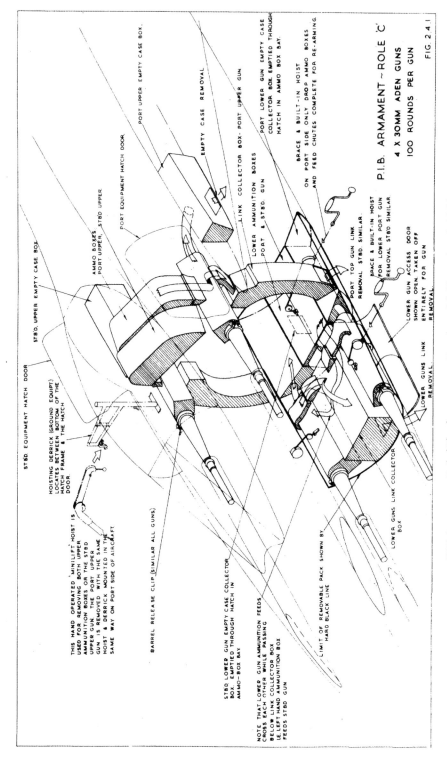

P1B Armament-Role 'C' – four cannon, Brochure 26, November 5, 1954.

consistent modification standards was "an expensive and time wasting nightmare".

The integration task in itself turned out to have unexpected complications with Government Furnished Equipment. For instance, OR946 was expected to be supplied as an integrated suite of displays. Instead it was delivered as an assembly of independently developed items produced to uncoordinated and inconsistent tolerances requiring major extra work by EECo as part of its integration with the other elements of the system.

MISSILE INSTALLATION

During 1956, the theoretical basis for assessing supersonic performance underwent a major revision with the open publication of Richard Whitcomb's 'Area Rule' following its classified issue in the USA in 1954. This replaced the goal of minimising the aircraft's frontal area with a more refined approach aiming to achieve a smooth variation of cross-sectional area from nose to tail. Analysis showed that, fortuitously, the P1 measured up very well in this respect. Some schemes were drawn up to add bulges to the fuselage to get further improvement, but these were found to be unnecessary when the air-to-air missiles were in place.

Intriguingly, the more bulged nose of the two-seat trainers had this beneficial effect and made them better than the single-seat fighters in clean condition. On the other hand, the configurations preferred by the RAE, such as the Bristol Type 188 and the Air Defence Working Party fighter recommendations for OR329/F155T, required major revision.

By the end of 1955, favourable results from test firings of Blue Jay from de Havilland Venom and DH110 aircraft gave EECo confidence in the viability of the P1B fuselage mounting of the missile in spite of its proximity to the engine intake. Detailed design work now concentrated on this; although the search continued for somewhere to mount two more missiles; a wingtip installation was increasingly favoured.

Meanwhile, throughout the first half of 1956,

knowledge of the design, performance and proposed usage of Blue Jay Marks 2 and 3 increased. Speed and height limitations were clarified, although some aspects of the thermal sensitivity of the seeker and fuse windows still required investigation. It seemed clear that some of the design features of Blue Jay Mk3 were driven by the needs of aircraft other than P1.

During an EECo visit to de Havilland Propellers in April to discuss the aircraft manoeuvre demands for firing Blue Jay, de Havilland suggested that the most helpful improvement to Blue Jay would be a large increase in launch angle off to cope with turning targets—but the Ministry would not change the specification because it was believed that the current 20° was enough since the target would not manoeuvre or at least not enough to evade.

Ray Creasey led an EECo visit to RRE on May 30, 1956, to learn its views on future air-to-air missiles and AI radar. They were advised that UK air defence might not be able to rely on continental early warning. In that event, the shorter warning time from UK radars would mean that incoming bombers could only be intercepted early enough by fighters capable of front hemisphere attacks. Semi-active radar missiles could achieve this but such missiles would be larger than infra-red homing missiles. This was because target glint caused larger miss distances for radar guided weapons and this could also be exacerbated by jamming. Therefore a larger warhead was needed and hence a larger missile (a doubling of miss distance required a warhead eight times heavier).

Infra-red homing missiles were attractive for being smaller and lighter. RRE's main concern was with the seeker limitations. Front hemisphere attacks were impossible with the lead sulphide seeker but might be possible with the lead telluride unit. Calculations based on V-bomber targets above 30,000ft altitude had shown lead telluride seeker lock-on at 8000 yards at 90° angle off and 7000 yards at 120° off the target's tail. RRE's main reservation was the lack of knowledge about atmospheric attenuation. They described several trials that were planned which would finally give solid data on the performance of lead telluride seekers. It might well be that infra-red missiles would prove adequate for front hemisphere attack.

As to AI radar, RRE thought that future radars should operate in J-band and incorporate static-split for lock-on. They outlined the AI radar planned for the F155 which would be used with Red Hebe or Sparrow III. A final note was that AI 20 was to be used as a tail-warning radar for V-bombers.

On June 14, de Havilland Propellers visited EECo to find out about progress on design for wing-tip carriage of missiles in respect to mounting, jettisoning and slaving of the IR head to the AI radar. EECo explained that they would be pursuing the topic, especially in case it was necessitated by larger missile wings. Their main concern was that harmonisation and slaving problems might be caused by aero-elastic distortion during manoeuvres. At this time, however, the design of the new cambered wing leading edge was taking priority.

Throughout the period, 1954-1956, while working on the design of P8 to F155T, EECo had also been learning more about the clearly superior Blue Jay Mk4. In the longer term, it seemed to offer the most potential. It had been suggested as an affordable way of meeting OR329 in EECo's tender to F155T, but had been rejected by RAE as too optimistic about seeker performance. The firm returned to the idea in the context of F23 with a draft project note in June 1956. This picked up on the discussions with RRE in May.

The study showed that any realistic supersonic bomber would produce a signature that allowed Blue Jay with a lead telluride seeker to be fired at up to 150° off the target's tail. This would actually allow head-on interception if the missile was fired in snap-up mode from 10,000ft below the target. As a result, the alternative semi-active radar seeker suggested by RRE could be regarded as a second string.

By mid-year, enough detail was available about Blue Jay to start detailed flight trials plans for its integration on the Lightning. The Aeroplane & Armament Experimental Establishment (A&AEE) operational trials plan assumed that the missile would be a cleared item, but trials to date had only

been done with Sabre aircraft. High-speed trials were needed to clear it on P1 before the A&AEE tests. A meeting on July 11 laid out a schedule of trials for carriage, aiming and firing clearance and specified the aircraft, missile round types, radars and range facilities required. One prototype and four Development Batch aircraft were earmarked for trials ranging from carriage and handling, jettison and fixed-fin firings, through to integration with AI 20 and AI 23 after the actual AI integration work.

For this final phase, it was proposed that the 10th Development Batch aircraft would be used for combined AI 23 and Blue Jay target acquisition trials from November 1957 and the 13th DB aircraft for AI 20 and Blue Jay trials in early 1958. Most of the planning focused on Blue Jay Mk1 but it was proposed that the non-expendable test rounds should have interchangeable Mk1 and Mk2 front ends to allow testing of the effect of the different nose shapes. EECo was also asked to propose the tests needed for Blue Jay Mk2 to assess the requirement for TI rounds.

Wider discussion of the various developments of Blue Jay still continued. On August 8, 1956, EECo and de Havilland Propellers met with MoS including staff from GW(Air) and the RN Project Officer for the SR177. It was agreed that, for service by about 1961, only Blue Jay Marks 1 and 2 would be cleared (up to an altitude of 55,000ft, carriage at up to M1.8 and launch at up to M1.5). De Havilland stressed that these were design limits and that the missile could be used beyond these limits, albeit probably at lower efficiency. EECo accepted that Marks 1 and 2 still seemed a reasonable compromise for F23/49 versus subsonic targets but restricted to tail-chase attacks.

As to Blue Jay Marks 2A and 3, EECo again suggested that no time or effort should be wasted on 2A as it was designed for a very unlikely launch condition at the expense of reduced capability in more usual circumstances. They also questioned the value of Blue Jay Mk3 as currently proposed. Its main extra feature was bigger wings to raise the intercept altitude to 65,000ft but, since it was limited to tail-chase attacks, it was only of use against subsonic

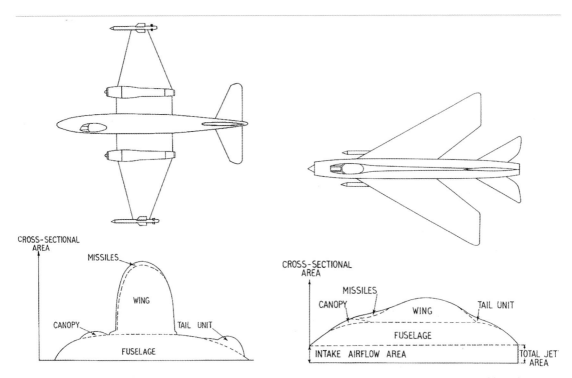

Richard Whitcomb's 'Area Rule' is that aerodynamic drag at supersonic speeds can be minimised by achieving a smooth distribution of total cross-section area from aircraft nose to tail. These diagrams from a Ray Creasey lecture show an aircraft with poor shape on the left and one with good characteristics on the right.

targets — most of which flew no higher than 55,000ft. The occasional subsonic photo-reconnaissance aircraft at higher altitudes could be dealt with by Blue Jay Mk2 since they lacked manoeuvrability at 60,000ft.

De Havilland now introduced ideas for an improved Blue Jay Mk3. They noted that recent tests of lead telluride seeker cells had confirmed the prospect of launches at up to 160° off the target's tail. EECo commented that interception studies had shown that, for firings from well below the target, the angle-off at launch never exceeded 160° even from head-on.

De Havilland work with EECo and Ferranti had shown that, if the seeker look angle was increased to 60° and slaved to the AI radar to allow lead angles of 20° or more, it could cater for 10,000ft snap-up firings. The RAF chair of the meeting, Wing Commander W B S Simpson GW1, suggested that this would

necessitate improved ground-controlled interception capabilities. EECo and the Navy representative said that, on the contrary, it was actually an easier task than setting up a tail-chase interception. The meeting concluded that Air Staff opinion should be sought while the three firms would develop a joint proposal on the way ahead.

Feedback from the Air Staff on August 17 was that Blue Jay Mk3 development as a tail-chase weapon should continue, but that de Havilland Propellers should submit proposals for the improved version. In fact, the three companies — EECo, de Havilland and Ferranti — had already met two days earlier to agree a common policy on Blue Jay Mk3. De Havilland introduced its latest proposals for the missile. It was a development of Blue Jay Marks 1 and 2 which would be capable of virtually all-round attack.

Two versions were being considered: a semi-active

Second prototype P1A WG763 doing gunfire tests against 'Jump Card' targets, January 1956.

radar-guided version for low-altitude and an infra-red homing type. The radar-guided weapon was required by the Royal Navy as it would not be affected by cloud. De Havilland regarded the IR version as the main one. It was expected to be capable of attack at angles-off of up to 155° by virtue of an improved guidance head and a look angle up to 60°. Launches at large lead angles would require slaving the seeker to the AI radar over much larger angles than hitherto. Subsequent discussion covered all aspects of the performance of the missile and the associated demands on the aircraft, fire control displays and radar.

EECo expressed the view that a special version of the P1 should be developed to fire the new missile. It would dispense with the other armament options. Fuselage mounting of the missile would be needed to minimize AI slaving errors. And a larger fin might be needed to counteract the influence of the larger missile wings. The PAS would be replaced by a dedicated steering display. It was agreed that the production date of 1961 set for the missile gave reasonable time to develop the new version of the P1, the radar

and computing equipment provided that development of the aircraft was firmly restricted to what was necessary to employ the new weapon.

De Havilland would produce a brochure giving more details of the missile and EECo would produce a brochure to cover the new weapon system as a whole.

Before August was out, however, de Havilland produced a detailed brochure of Blue Jay Mk4. EECo received a copy on September 17. It was prominently marked "not yet approved by the Ministry of Supply". As with Blue Jay Mk3, it proposed radar and IR guided versions.

These were based on assumed operational requirements. Firstly, that UK air defence between 1960 and at least 1965 would depend on the English Electric F23 and the Saunders Roe P177, equipped with AI 23 and armed with Blue Jay, intercepting targets flying at Mach 1.3 or more at altitudes up to 65,000ft. Secondly, the Royal Navy would be relying on the DH110, equipped with AI 18 and armed with Blue Jay, intercepting subsonic targets, perhaps in cloud, at altitudes up to 55,000ft. Interception with tail

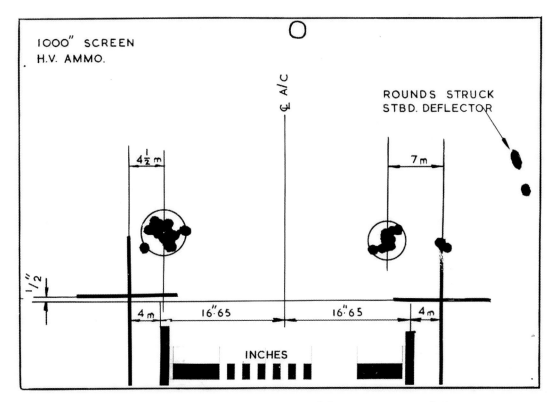

An early Jump Card showing the pattern of impacts around the aim points. Note the impacts at upper right from rounds that have tumbled after striking the protective blast plate near the gun muzzle.

chase Blue Jay Mk1 required accurate GCI control and would be of little use against supersonic targets or subsonic targets employing carcinatron jamming. Blue Jay Mk4 was therefore intended to provide an all-round attack capability.

The IR version was for the F23 and P177. It would employ the new more sensitive seeker with a wider look angle and have larger wings, giving an altitude clearance from 15,000ft to 65,000ft. The radar version, with an X-band continuous wave (CW) homing head supported by a developed AI 18 radar, would meet the Navy's needs. It would retain the original size wings and altitude clearance from sea level to 55,000ft. (An addendum to the brochure in July 1957 would re-designate the radar version as Blue Jay Mk5).

The brochure described in great detail the design, performance and operational employment of the missile. The section on fire control detailed the error

budgets involved in IR missile harmonization and slaving to AI 23 radar in the P1 installation. More than two dozen diagrams showed the size and shape of the firing zones for a wide range of target and fighter speeds and altitudes. It also laid out a development programme running from 1957 to service entry in 1961.

A section on aircraft platforms listed not only a developed P1, a developed P177 and a developed (Mk20) DH110 but also the N113 and a developed Javelin. The N113 would carry the low-altitude version with an IR seeker. The developed Javelin could use the low-altitude IR version or, with a suitable radar, the low-altitude radar version. It was also noted that the DH110 could use the low altitude IR version as well as the radar version. Each version, however, would require different equipment in the aircraft.

EECo returned to promoting the advantages of

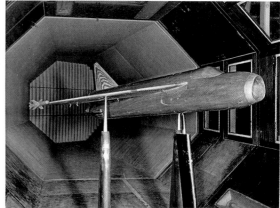

**Two views of the P1A model in the 9 x 7ft wind tunnel during tests
to find suitable locations for carrying extra missiles.**

Blue Jay Mk4 for the F23 in a brochure issued in October 1956. This showed the significant benefits from head-on interceptions compared to tail-chase engagements. It analysed the potential target characteristics of bombers and reconnaissance aircraft and presented results of interception studies against a Mach 1.3 target at 60,000ft altitude and subsonic targets. These showed that, against a subsonic target, front hemisphere attack with Blue Jay Mk4 resulted in an interception 30nm further from the coast than the tail-chase with Blue Jay Mk1. Against the Mach 1.3 target, Blue Jay Mk4 allowed interception at distances that were only possible against subsonic targets with Blue Jay Mk1. OR 268 Issue 6 was circulated on December 31, 1956.

RISING COSTS

While EECo was grappling with the integration of two alternative AI radars and several possible missiles, the Treasury again had cost concerns. In response to a query about a doubling of costs between 1955 and 1956, N Craig of MoS wrote to J E Herbecq at the Treasury on January 22, 1957, detailing the latest cost estimates for the design and construction of the 20 aircraft of the development batch.

The cost had originally been estimated at £5m, then £1.5m had been added in July 1955 to cover the design task. This was then raised to £2m in the 1955 Vote Letter Supplement (VLS). Now, in the 1956 VLS, the total cost was estimated at £13m comprising £6.8m for design, mock-ups, test components and the flight programme plus £6.2m for production. The cost rise was attributed to production difficulties due to the complexity of the nose fuselage and the duplication of design effort and flight testing to cater for two different sets of AI equipment and an interim flight instrument set.

The Treasury was taken aback, as shown in an exchange of scribbled notes on February 5. Herbecq to Armstrong: "This is a good example of how R&D projects can get completely out of control… This is in part due to the inclusion of work to which reference was not made earlier (we are not told why)… One reason for this is that two sets of AI equipment are to be incorporated… we ought to get the Ministry of Supply round and thoroughly examine them on the course of development of this aircraft during the past 18 months."

Armstrong to Herbecq: "I must say that I do not think the Ministry of Supply letter of 22.1.57 adds up to a justification for the increase from £2m to £6.8m on the design work. I find it hard to believe that the duplication of AI sets was not known about earlier; I have certainly known for several months, from the electronics side, that we were spending money on AI 20 development… as well as on AI 23…"

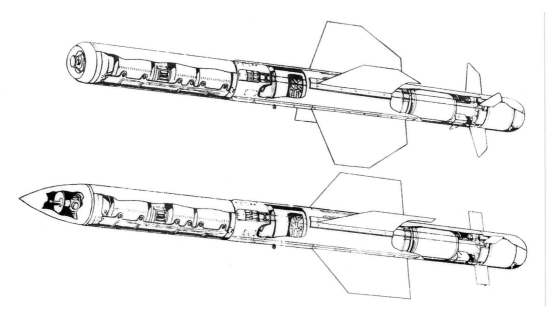

Blue Jay Mk4 as of August 1956. Top: high altitude, infra-red guided version; bottom: medium altitude radar guided version.

English Electric, de Havilland Propellers, Ferranti and Elliotts jointly presented a set of proposals for developments of the P1 on January 30, 1957. In their contribution, de Havilland again promoted the benefits of the lead telluride seeker and the improved characteristics of Blue Jay Mk4. They also suggested that cancellation of Blue Jay Mk3 would allow earlier service introduction of the Mk4, albeit about a year later than planned for the Mk3.

CUTS AND CANCELLATIONS

There were major defence changes under way by 1957. Three years earlier, in July 1954, the Chiefs of Staff had issued a new Defence Policy. It responded to the growing threat from nuclear weapons and the increasing capabilities of ballistic and guided missiles. Faced also with Government demands for reductions in the defence budget, it questioned the value of many of the defence equipment programmes and led to a series of force cuts and project cancellations.

The Vickers Supermarine Type 545 Developed Swift (to F105D2) was reduced to a research programme with the cancellation of the second prototype on November 9, 1954, and later cancelled completely. At a meeting with the Air Staff and the RAE on December 12, 1955, DGTD(A) announced that CA proposed to cancel F153D—the Thin-wing Javelin. This would save money not only on the aircraft itself but also on Red Dean and some developments of the Olympus engine.

The RAF, with full support from the RAE, argued strongly for its retention, saying that it was the only option to provide all-weather, front hemisphere interception of high-altitude targets until F155 entered service. The only other options against these targets were F23/49 with rocket boost or the Rocket Fighter. Neither of these had full all-weather capability or the ability to carry Red Dean. Furthermore, development of Red Dean was a key step towards Red Hebe.

The Thin-wing Javelin lingered on until it was finally cancelled on June 21, 1956. At that time, Gloster was preparing to send a basic F153D model via RAE Bedford to NASA Langley in the USA for wind tunnel tests. Gloster's own low-speed wind tunnel was not expected to be operational until early 1958. A report to the Gloster board meeting

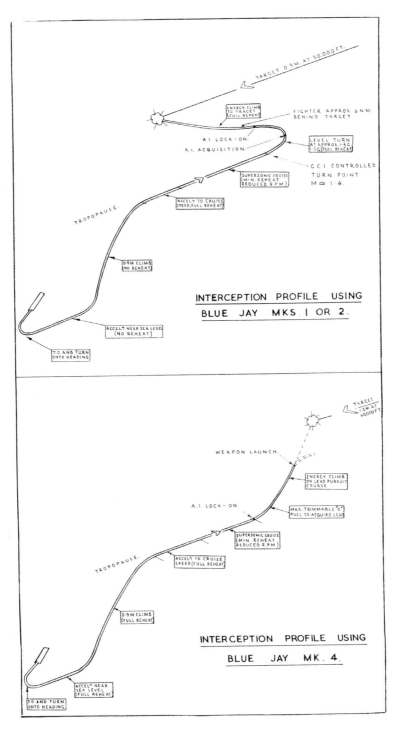

Diagrams from Brochure 37, October 1956, showing the earlier interception achievable with head-on firings of Blue Jay Mk4 (bottom) compared to tail chase firings with Blue Jay Mk1 or 2 (top).

The prototype P1B, XA847, on its first flight, April 4, 1957.

on September 20 stated that all work on F153D had ceased following cancellation of the contract. The reasons for cancellation had never been made clear. Furthermore, "In the absence of any clearly defined Air Staff policy regarding fighters, with no apparent prospect of a call for new types, concentration in the Design Office is now on existing Javelin and its development possibilities."

Now, on February 21, 1957, in the light of the dominance of ballistic missiles as the future strategic threat plus the increasing capabilities of surface-to-air guided weapons (SAGW) and in accordance with the 1954 Defence Policy, attention turned to longer-term air defence. On the advice of the Air Staff, the Air Council agreed to cancel several major aircraft projects. These included the Fairey 'Delta 3' to F155 (OR329) and the Saunders-Roe SR177 to F177 (OR337). The F23 was to be retained and developed to its useful limit.

The main development focus for air defence would

be long-range SAGW including an anti-ballistic missile capability. On March 11, DOR(A) drafted a letter to the MoS explaining the reasons for the cancellations. These cancellations would then feature prominently in the Defence White Paper presented by Duncan Sandys in April.

The day after the Air Council meeting, and as yet unaffected by its decisions, Issue 4 of F23/49 was finally circulated. Although the Operational Requirement only asked for armament with Blue Jay; the specification called for Blue Jay Mk1 or Mk2.

The third prototype and first P1B flew on April 4 and went supersonic during the flight. That same month, EECo produced a detailed brochure, 'P1B Interceptor Fighter—Weapon System to Specification F23/49 (Issues 3 and 4) with Mixed Power Plant'. The main text gave a detailed description of the aircraft with the specified Blue Jay armament and presented performance for tail-chase attacks. The

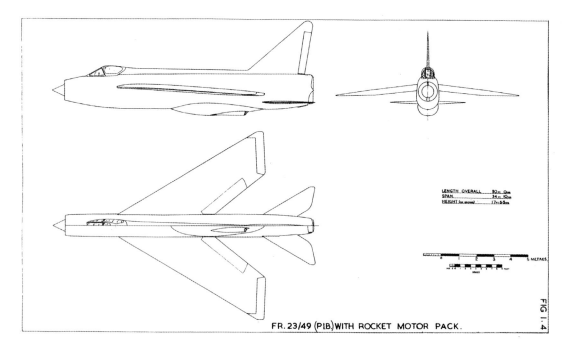

P1B still being proposed with rocket booster pack option, Brochure 40, April 1957.

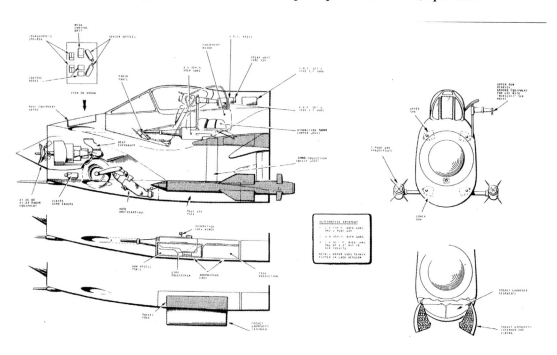

P1B nose layout showing armament options, Brochure 40, April 1957.
Note that the radar is now labelled as "AI 20 or AI 23".

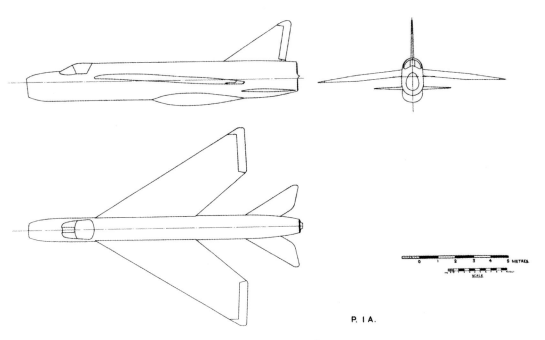

P1A, Brochure 44, September 1958.

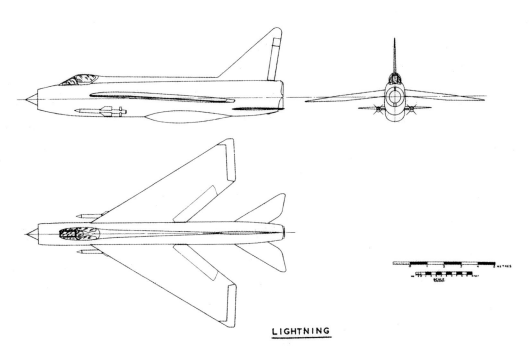

Lightning, Brochure 44, September 1958 (P1B has now been named Lightning).

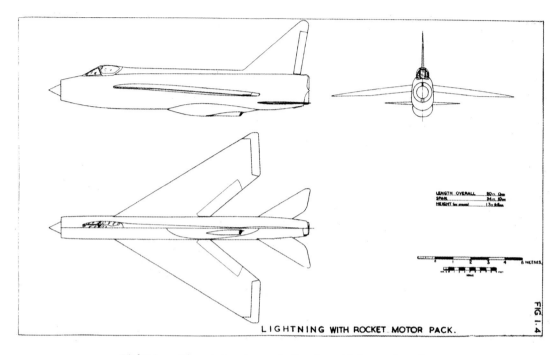

FIG 1.4

LIGHTNING WITH ROCKET MOTOR PACK.

Lightning with rocket motor pack, Brochure 44, September 1958.

maximum speed was limited to Mach 1.7 pending further investigation and development. The use of rocket boost was shown to raise the ceiling to above 65,000ft via zoom manoeuvres with a note that recent testing of the Napier rocket motors had produced 50% more thrust than assumed in the study. Both AI 20 and AI 23 were still presented as the radar options, but only AI 23 was described in detail.

Since it was not part of the official requirement or specification, discussion of collision-course interception with Blue Jay Mk4 was confined to a section on 'Future Developments'. This also addressed the problems of intercepting bombers using 100-mile range powered bombs, bombers using ECM and targets flying at 60,000ft or more. It was suggested that the problem of bombers cruising at supersonic speed, and not just short dashes, was sufficiently far in the future to be left until later in the fighter's development.

AI 20 had in effect been cancelled for P1B on March 13 when instruction was given for work to cease on all aspects of AI 20 except the V-bomber application (i.e. the 'Red Steer' tail-warning radar).

In light of this decision, on March 21, the Treasury wrote to the MoS requesting that, since a funding increase requested on January 22 had cited the need to incorporate and test two different AI radars, could the MoS now inform them of the cost savings resulting from the cancellation of AI 20? The immediate reply was that the development flying programme was being revised and it would be several weeks before there would be an answer. In the event, the substantive reply was delayed until September 19. This was presumably because of the new demands on the P1 laid down at a meeting on June 24, following the April White Paper. The result was a request to increase the programme funding from £13m to £14.6m. The £1.6m increase took into account £200,000 saved as a result of cancelling AI 20.

As 1957 drew to a close, the way ahead for P1 seemed clear to the Air Staff and the Ministry of Supply. The fighter would be produced in three or possibly four variants. Mark 1 would be an interim design, Mark 2 would introduce the definitive cockpit display system to OR946 and Mark 3 would bring in an all-round attack capability with Blue Jay Mk4. A possible Mark 4 aircraft would have more powerful Rolls-Royce RB133 engines but would require a redesigned fuselage.

At this time, however, only Marks 1 and 2 had Treasury funding and funding would continue to be tight. For instance, there was no R&D money for Blue Jay Mk4 for P1. This was partly because the SR177 rocket fighter was still absorbing R&D funds since, even though it was no longer required by the RAF or RN, there was concern about unemployment on the Isle of Wight and there remained a remote possibility of German interest. Beyond this, there were still voices in Government and official circles calling for the abolition of Fighter Command and the complete cancellation of the P1 programme. Political and financial battles lay ahead.

At least the way ahead for Blue Jay would finally be settled by mid-1958. By then there had been 15 R&D firings of Blue Jay Mk1 (eight hits) and 20 acceptance trials firings (13 hits) plus two firings of Blue Jay Mk2 — but this would now only be used as a test vehicle for Blue Jay Mk4. Blue Jay Mk3 and Mk5 had been cancelled and would no longer be delaying Blue Jay Mk 4. Redesign of the control system had overcome the low altitude limitations on the Mk4 and various other design enhancements were in hand.

This apart, much other work was still required with the Lightning prototypes, the development batch and beyond to introduce the numerous items of equipment and to integrate the system. Nevertheless, within a year it would be agreed that the Lightning would not only be a key element of UK air defence but would also be deployed to the front line of NATO in Germany. It would take another three years to get the Mark 1 into service and seven years to get to nearly the full potential with the Mark 3; but Lightning would serve on the front line for 28 years until it finally retired in 1988.

Lightning Projects

Chapter 5

WHAT LIGHTNING MIGHT HAVE BEEN (P6 AND P8)

Although the main design effort for Lightning would be devoted to developing the basic airframe and weapon system to meet the official requirements and specifications, some advanced project studies continued with two objectives. The first was to address the operational limitations of Lightning's sensors and weapons. The second was to explore the possibility of expanding Lightning's role as had been done with earlier fighters.

The Lightning fighter is commonly also referred to by the English Electric project number 'P1'. But, in fact, there are 15 project numbers between P1 and P34 associated with the Lightning. These are listed in Annex 1. Some refer to development steps in the core programme as described in the preceding section. Others relate to studies to extend the aircraft's capabilities beyond the scope of the official requirement. The following chapters describe some of the latter studies together with some proposed developments that were never given 'P' numbers.

These studies fall broadly into five categories. First, early studies in response to other official requirements that presented opportunities to re-direct the main line of development. Secondly, studies to extend the basic aircraft's capabilities including additional roles. Later, these studies would be a basis for proposed export variants. Then came proposals to improve the basic fighter capability with new sensors and weapons. Finally, with the advent of the variable geometry or 'swing-wing' concept there were proposals to exploit this in Lightning developments.

Most of these studies took place in the ten years following the 1957 Defence White Paper. As with the core programme, the investment decisions for these various developments were affected by the other contemporary programmes.

In the early stages, these included the many programmes highlighted in the preceding sections. Later, during Lightning's long period of RAF service, there would be the P1154, AFVG, McDonnell Douglas Phantom, and Tornado ADV to be considered.

Before describing the later attempts to improve the Lightning's capabilities, we will return to two missed opportunities that were mentioned earlier when describing the main development thread.

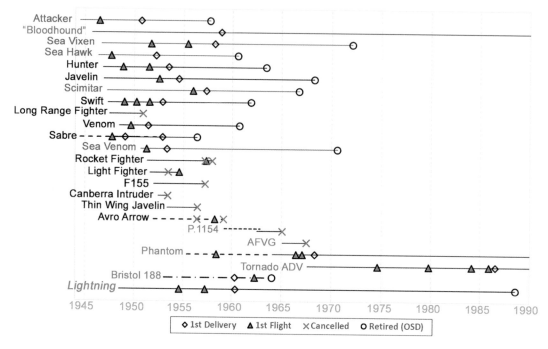

This chart includes the main additional projects that would compete with Lightning for future development funds: P1154, Phantom, AFVG, Tornado ADV.

ENGLISH ELECTRIC P6

During 1952, as the P1 design was still being developed, the F23/49 fighter (P1) and the ER103 research aircraft (Fairey FD2) were regarded respectively as Mach 1.5 and Mach 1.3 aeroplanes. It was recognised that they had the potential to be developed to a Mach 2 capability. Nevertheless, believing that future fighters, bombers and reconnaissance aircraft might be aimed at speeds of Mach 2 or more, the RAE made the case for a new research aircraft to be designed from the outset as a Mach 2 vehicle.

The RAE's ideas for ideal Mach 2 aircraft designs were presented in June 1952 in report Aero 2462. This proposed a twin engine configuration with a long slender fuselage, thin straight wing, a high tail-plane and the engines in mid-wing nacelles. The Ministry of Supply published an appropriate specification, ER134T, in December 1952 and this was circulated to industry with an Invitation to Tender in January 1953.

As mentioned previously, EECo's initial response was a development of the F23/49 design with the more powerful Sapphire Sa7 engines. Designated P6, it was included in the F23/49 brochure dated February 5, 1953, as offering a different route for the fighter project. The main response to ER134T was delivered in a brochure dated May 15, 1953. This proposed a more modest F23/49 derivative plus three new designs. The modified F23/49 retained the Sa5 engines of the P1 but with 25% re-heat boost and convergent-divergent nozzles.

P6/1 was based on the P1 configuration but with a single Rolls-Royce RB106 engine. P6/2 was based on the original P6 design with Sa7 engines but with the addition of convergent-divergent nozzles. Finally, bowing towards the RAE's design preferences, P6B was a completely new design with straight wings, Sa7 engines in mid-wing nacelles and a high tail-plane. A brief check on replacing the 'chevron' wing with a delta showed no areas of improvement but

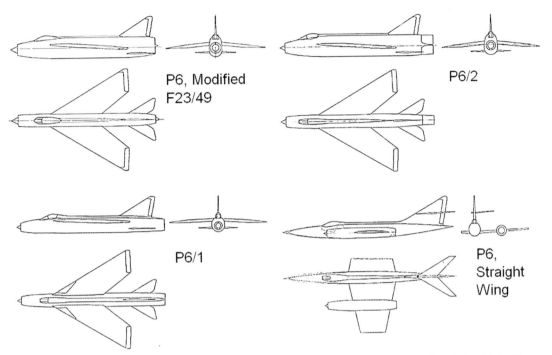

The four P6 options presented in response to Specification ER134T in a brochure dated May 15, 1953.

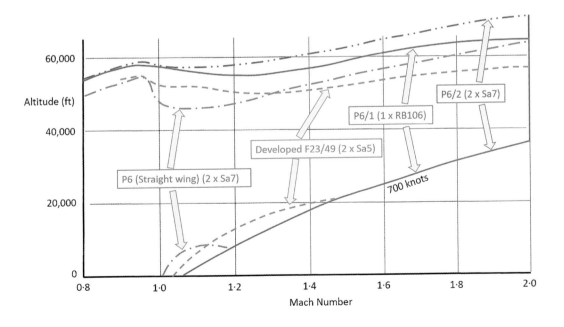

Graph showing the different flight envelopes for the four P6 options, May 15, 1953.

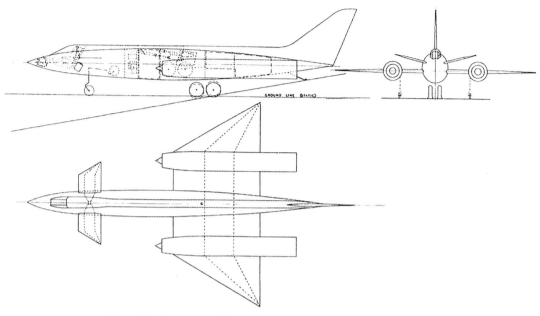

The radical new canard design for P6 proposed in September 1953.

rather a loss of performance in speed, ceiling and climb. All of the designs had flight envelopes limited at Mach 2 but clearly showing the potential to achieve higher speeds.

EECo presented the single-engine P6/1 as the most attractive option. Although not achieving quite the level of performance of the P6/2, it offered a simpler and cheaper solution. The swept wing offered better altitude and manoeuvre performance across the speed range compared to a straight wing. The retention of the wings and many other parts of the P1 made it much cheaper to design and build compared to a totally new design. Pending its development, it was suggested that the modified F23/49 proposal offered a quick way forward for an initial exploration of the Mach 2 flight regime and its attendant structural heating problems.

The straight wing P6B was viewed unfavourably by EECo. In a straight line, at a speed of Mach 2, the straight wing performed as well as any other. The aircraft, however, was heavy. It had poor transonic and altitude performance and had severe stability, control and aeroelastic problems that would need

considerable research investigation themselves. Nevertheless, in view of RAE's preferences, EECo continued to explore straight wing designs.

In September 1953, they presented a radical canard design. By this time, however, the RAE had dismissed EECo's assessment of straight wings as being too pessimistic. Also the goal was now to research speeds up to Mach 2.5 to support the development of the planned supersonic fighter, bomber and reconnaissance types.

Certain that a straight-winged design with wing mounted engines was the right solution, RAE favoured the Armstrong Whitworth and Bristol submissions. These were very similar. The design conference preferred the AW, but the choice finally went to the Bristol Type 188 because of the company's lower workload as minuted by CS(A) on October 7, 1953. The original plan was for two aircraft, the first with an alloy wing and the second with an experimental steel wing, for a total cost of £2.5m. First flight was expected to be by 1957.

The development proved very complex, delaying progress and raising cost. Extra prototypes were

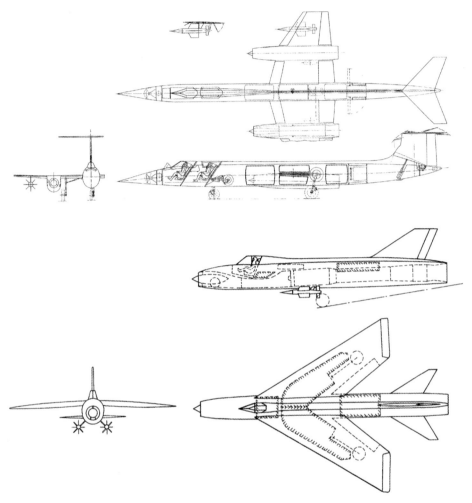

These layouts show RAE's suggestions as to what were good and bad configurations for a future Mach 2 Fighter as presented in the report of the Air Defence Committee Working Party, April 1954. The upper configuration was presented as desirable; the lower one as unsuitable. (TNA AVIA 6/19287)

ordered and then cancelled. By December 1955, the cost estimate had risen to £7m and doubts were raised as to whether the aircraft would fly in time to be of any use to other programmes. By May 1958, cost predictions were rising to £10m and the OR329 and OR330 projects that were intended to benefit from it had been cancelled.

First flight was achieved on April 14, 1962. The aircraft fell far short of its goals in speed and

endurance. Its maximum speed was only Mach 1.88. The two prototypes had cost £14m for the airframe alone. In total the programme cost about £20m. Flying lasted less than two years. Sir George Edwards of Vickers said that nothing was learned from the Type 188 except "not to build aeroplanes like that". Before this lesson was learnt, however, the thinking behind the ER134T programme was also driving the OR329 fighter programme.

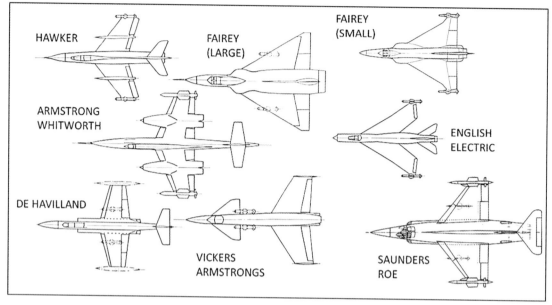

A plan view showing the competing F155T tender submissions to the same scale.

ENGLISH ELECTRIC P8

A conference in December 1951 about replacing the Hunter and Swift had proposed an aircraft with a speed of up to Mach 1.8. A draft OR was prepared in February 1952. This proved controversial and, after a year of meetings and papers on fighter requirements and concepts, a completely new draft, OR329 for a "high altitude supersonic interceptor", was circulated in February 1953—followed by a second draft in November and three more in early 1954.

A sanitized version of the fifth draft was circulated to 11 firms including EECo on March 19, 1954. The requirement was finally issued in August 1954 and was sent to the 11 firms in October. In the same month, a draft specification, F155T, was circulated. It was eventually issued on January 15, 1955 and eight firms were invited to tender. A meeting with the tendering firms on April 5 led to amendments to OR329 in July revising the performance goals and in August changing the title to "all weather interceptor". A second issue of F155T on July 5, 1955, relaxed the performance and weapon load requirements.

A key aspect in all this was the framing of the requirement and specification as being for a "weapon system". Thus, the aircraft Operational Requirement included as addenda five other ORs covering weapons, radar and equipment. In 1956, concerned that only lip service was being paid to the weapon system concept, DOR(B) drafted a single replacement for these five addenda to emphasise the need for all the elements to be considered together.

During 1954, the broad development of the specification was influenced by the concurrent work of an Air Defence Committee Working Party chaired by Arnold Hall of RAE. This was exploring the future needs for all elements of the UK Air Defence System. The fighter aspects were studied by the RAE and reported in April 1954 as "Air Defence against High Altitude Bombers by Mach 2 Fighters". It was also published later as RAE Report Aero 2513.

Drawing on the work for the Mach 2 research aircraft, it proposed a twin engine fighter configuration similar to the RAE ideal research aircraft from report Aero 2462 and the Bristol Type 188 selected against ER134T. In contrast, it also presented a layout clearly based on EECo's P6/1 submission to ER134T as being unsatisfactory. The RAE design was

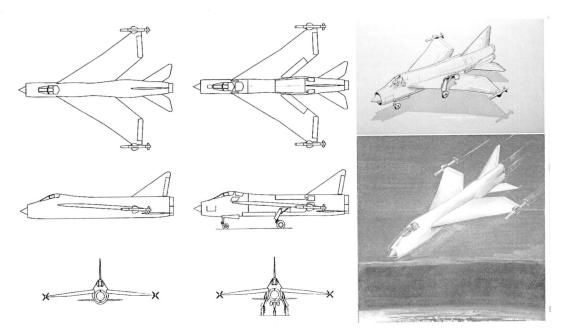

English Electric P8 from the tender brochure, October 4, 1955.

assessed to be lighter and with better performance than the Lightning-like design. A subsequent RAE study about a year later revised the design to meet the F155T specification. This doubled the weight and changed from two to four engines.

Of the eight companies invited, seven submitted tenders in October 1955. These varied widely in their response—some were sceptical of the possibility of meeting even the new, relaxed specification. At the other extreme, Saunders-Roe believed it could satisfy the original, more challenging specification. These various responses were received differently by the RAF and the MoS. The Air Staff had asked that the aircraft be kept as small and cheap as possible. They also asked the firms to consider the totality of the weapon system and the nature of the operational task and to propose any innovative solutions that might offer a more economical approach.

By contrast, the MoS believed that the only fair and practical way to assess the tenders was by ranking them rigidly according to the extent to which they met all the demands of the revised specification. This included meeting all the performance goals while carrying a crew of two, a large radar and two huge radar-guided Red Hebe air-to-air missiles.

Hawkers and EECo were the leading sceptics. Both believed that meeting the performance goals while carrying Red Hebe would be unaffordable. Hawkers designed what they believed was the smallest fighter capable of meeting the performance goals while carrying the much smaller Blue Vesta missile. The design was capable of carrying Red Hebe, but with reduced performance. They did little to explore the weapon system aspects as they believed that the procurement system left them little ability to influence the equipment choice and design.

EECo, on the other hand, were credited with having a strong grasp of the weapon system concept and did extensive studies to show that adequate role performance could be achieved with a single seat aircraft armed with Blue Jay Mk4 (Blue Vesta) missiles. The proposed aircraft, P8, was essentially a derivative of the P1B but with RB126 engines instead of RA24s. It had a fuselage mounted undercarriage and wing-tip missile carriage. Its all-up weight was almost the same as the P1B. This choice of development route was also seen as offering the realistic prospect of meeting the required early service date.

The contrast between these proposals and those of the other firms bemused the Air Staff. They noted that the confidence of the various firms as to their ability to meet the specification was inversely proportional to their experience of building this type of aeroplane. The competing designs differed widely in size and shape.

At the tender review conference, some of the Air Staff favoured basing the choices for the way ahead on the general capabilities of the firms rather than the specific designs submitted. They particularly mentioned English Electric as first choice. The Ministry of Supply, however, insisted that the agreed tendering process meant that the choice must be based strictly on whether the designs met the specification in detail.

The initial down-selection ruled out the Saunders-Roe proposal as unnecessarily heavy and complex, being aimed at the earlier specification. It was twice the weight of the EECo P8 when empty and three times as heavy when loaded. Conversely, the Hawker and EECo proposals were ruled out as failing to satisfy so many aspects of the specification. Furthermore, the RAE believed that EECo were being too optimistic about the performance of the Blue Vesta seeker and hence the use of infra-red weapons for front hemisphere attack.

The choice eventually narrowed down to the larger of the two designs submitted by Fairey and the Armstrong Whitworth design. The Fairey design drew upon the company's experience with the ER103 research aircraft (FD2). The Armstrong Whitworth design, with its straight wing and four podded jet engines plus rocket motor, was very like the RAE's own suggestion to meet F155T. After the next phase of work, the final choice was the large Fairey delta, before the programme was cancelled in 1957.

When the EECo P8 was rejected, the Air Staff requested that funding be found to continue it as a Lightning development—but no money could be spared. Lightning would eventually be developed to perform interceptions with Red Top in the manner proposed for P8, but without the possible benefits of the other design features of P8.

Chapter 6

EARLY DEVELOPMENT PROPOSALS

Even before the 1957 Defence White Paper left Lightning as the only advanced fighter project for the RAF, industry had already begun to look at possible developments to widen its roles and capabilities. As mentioned earlier, on January 30, 1957, English Electric, de Havilland Propellers, Ferranti and Elliotts jointly presented a set of proposals for developments of the P1. At this time, the baseline was P1B fitted with Rolls-Royce RA24R engines plus two Napier Scorpion rocket motors (awaiting an ITP). It was designed to perform 'lead-pursuit' interceptions, employing AI 23 or, as an interim measure, AI 20 and Blue Jay Mk1 or Mk2 or Sidewinder guided missiles, changing to Blue Jay Mk4 as soon as possible. Unguided weapon options included four Aden cannon or two Aden to supplement the guided weapons, or two Aden plus 48 unguided rockets.

The development proposals were covered by four EECo project numbers: P11, P15, P18 and P19. These comprised a two-seat trainer variant and three operational enhancements. P11 retained the original P1 wing planform while the other three incorporated the proposed addition of an extended, cambered, outboard leading-edge. This was already under test on

the P1A and was eventually adopted for later marks of Lightning.

P11 was the two-seat trainer. It had started as a response to OR318 for an advanced trainer in 1953. A tandem seat design was proposed in 1955 but it had now evolved to a side-by-side cockpit, some of the space being found by deleting the upper pair of Aden cannon.

P15 was a photo-reconnaissance variant. The cameras were to be fitted in a pack to substitute for the weapons pack. Two alternative packs were also offered—each with six F95 cameras to give forward and lateral oblique and near-vertical settings. The two packs differed only in the camera focal lengths, one set being 4in and the other 12in. It also had wing-tip overload fuel tanks to extend the radius of action.

P18 was described as a tactical bomber. It is shown configured for the strike role with a single 'Target Marker' (Red Beard nuclear weapon) mounted tangentially under the fuselage.

P19 was an improved fighter variant. It proposed new, more powerful Rolls-Royce engines such as the RB133 with convergent-divergent nozzles and mass flow control plus weapon system improvements

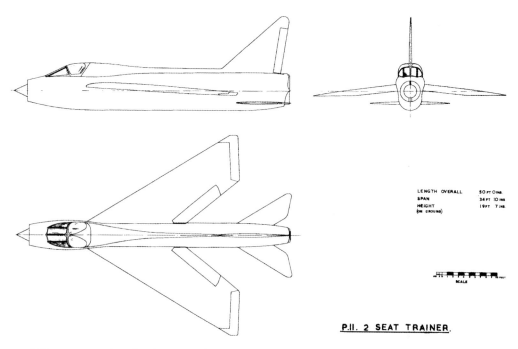

P11 two-seat trainer development of P1, January 30, 1957. Note the early standard wing.

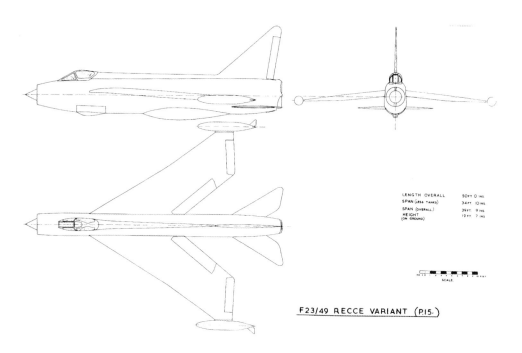

P15 photo reconnaissance development of P1, January 30, 1957. Note
the developed wing with outboard leading edge camber.

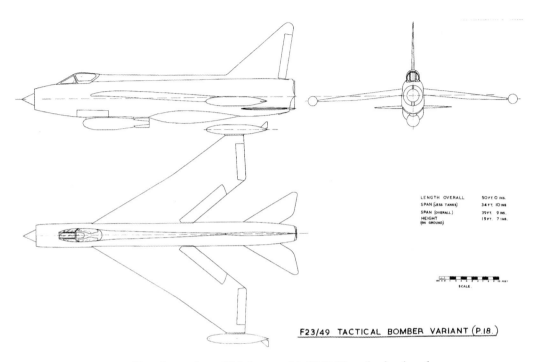

P18 tactical bomber variant of P1, January 30, 1957. Note the developed wing and the single 'Target Marker'/Red Beard munition.

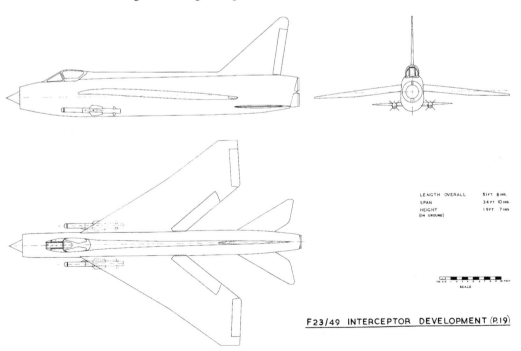

P19 interceptor development of P1, January 30, 1957. Note the developed wing and Blue Jay Mk4 armament.

offering a front hemisphere interception capability. This was based on ideas already offered for the P8 to F155T in 1955 and a P1B development proposed in 1956. It included a J-band version of AI 23 and armament of Blue Jay Mk4 or Sparrow 2.

The contributions from the equipment companies focused on the P19 fighter. De Havilland Propellers detailed the seeker and performance improvements for Blue Jay Mk4. In particular, the company demonstrated the increased sensitivity of a lead telluride seeker to replace the lead sulphide seeker of Blue Jay

Mk1 (Firestreak). Ferranti described the features and benefits of the proposed J-band version of AI 23; Elliotts proposed the changes to the autopilot that were needed to go from a 'lead-pursuit' to a 'lag-collision' intercept mode.

Any official response seems to have been overtaken by events with the publication of the Defence White Paper in April 1957. The main line of Lightning development for the RAF would focus on the interceptor fighter role. Ideas for widening the role capabilities would, for the moment, be deferred.

Chapter 7

GROUND ATTACK

The P18 Tactical bomber had been proposed at a time when the P1 was still expected to have a relatively short service life as an interceptor pending the deployment of the F155. However, following the 1957 Defence White Paper and the decision that the P1 should be the only interceptor, thoughts turned to interpretation of the instruction that it should be developed to its full potential.

The initial focus was on establishing the route to achieving an all-round attack capability in the interceptor role. By early 1958, however, considering the implications of providing a successor to the Hunter and Swift, a brochure was prepared outlining some proposals for further developments of the P1B. As well as summarising the way ahead for the interceptor with Blue Jay Mk4, new displays, data link and uprated engines; it proposed ground attack and photo reconnaissance variants.

The reconnaissance variant was very like the P15 design with a camera pack replacing the armaments pack under the nose and extra fuel in under-wing and wing-tip drop tanks. The ground attack proposal suggested using the existing armament options of guns and 2in rockets in an air-to-ground mode

with the 'Airpass' system (AI 23 & PAS) modified to provide air-to-ground target range. Extra fuel could be carried as per the photo reconnaissance fit or the under-wing drop tanks could be replaced by extra pods of rockets.

As a further provision to extend the aircraft's range, a retractable air-to-air refuelling probe would be fitted on the left side of the nose. Finally, for maximum ferry range, a removable fuel tank could be fitted in the weapons pack bay. This, together with the under-wing and wing-tip tanks would raise the maximum fuel load from 974 gallons to 1524 gallons. All of these developments could be applied to either the single or two seat aircraft.

Following further design and wind tunnel work, a revised brochure was issued in January 1959. The main changes were pylons over the wing instead of under the wing and a detachable under-wing flight refuelling probe instead of the retractable nose unit.

Several key topics had to be addressed to take the design ideas forward. Air-to-ground weapon delivery would require new aiming facilities. These in turn would be affected by the choice of weapons and the aircraft manoeuvres required to deliver them.

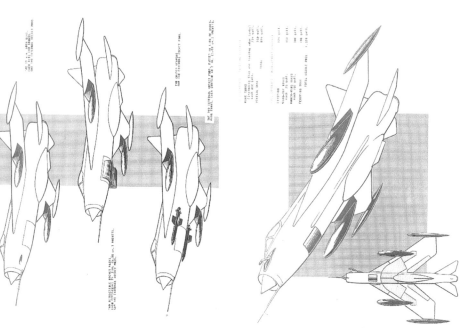

Configurations proposed and starting to be tested in the wind tunnel as shown in the Lightning Development brochure, 1958. The underwing stores include rocket pods and fuel tanks. Note the maximum fuel plus in-flight refuelling provision for ferry purposes in the bottom picture.

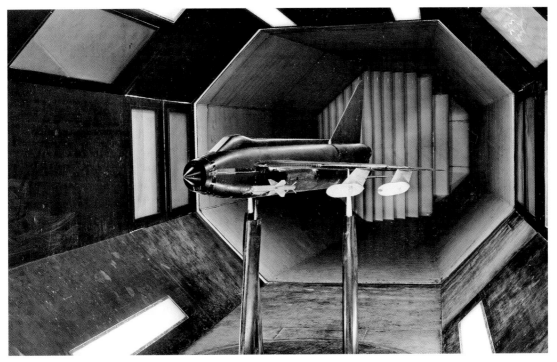

Wind tunnel testing of underwing stores, June 1958.

These extra manoeuvre demands and the increased proportion of flight time at low altitude would require structural strengthening to cope with the changed load spectrum and its effect on airframe fatigue life.

Alec Atkin and Tony Simmons of English Electric Aviation visited Ferranti to discuss a ground attack system for the Lightning on January 26, 1959. Various systems were discussed, with Ferranti anxious to retain responsibility for all fire control and weapon aiming. The company favoured a two-seat arrangement and suggested methods of navigation and a system such as Blue Parrot for weapon aiming and perhaps blind attack. (Blue Parrot was the maritime target acquisition radar being developed for the Royal Navy's Buccaneer). In weapons discussions, Ferranti confirmed that, as far as was known, 'Target Marker 1' and 'Red Beard' were one and the same and outlined typical accuracy requirements. Detailed weapon aiming discussion, however, focused on the use of the smaller air-to-air nuclear

weapon 'Genie' in an air-to-ground mode.

The idea of using Genie was taken up by EEA (English Electric Aviation) for a brief study of Lightning developments for low-level strike. A short memorandum on October 28 described four aircraft configurations. Two engine options were considered (RA24 and RB163) and in each case two aircraft configurations—one with the normal Lightning wing and one with much smaller, clipped wings.

Large pods with extra fuel were proposed and consideration was given to a twin-wheel undercarriage for soft field operation. In all cases, armament was a single Genie semi-recessed into a revised ventral pack. Only the RB163 variant with the normal wing was seen to have any promise and even this presented intake and reheat problems. In the event, only the revised ventral tank and weapon installation was taken forward into future studies.

Official interest picked up at the beginning of 1960. The Chief of Air Staff, Air Chief Marshal Sir Thomas Pike, speaking to Lord Caldecote, asked

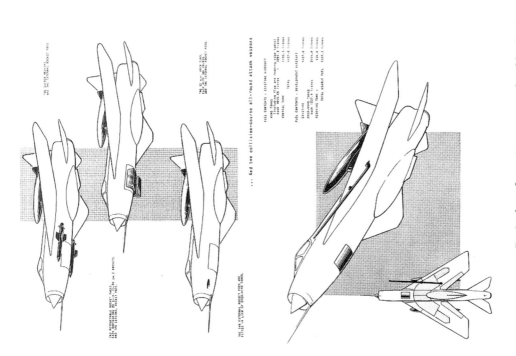

Revised configurations proposed and beginning testing as shown in the second issue of the Lightning Development brochure, January 1959. Note the change from underwing to overwing store carriage.

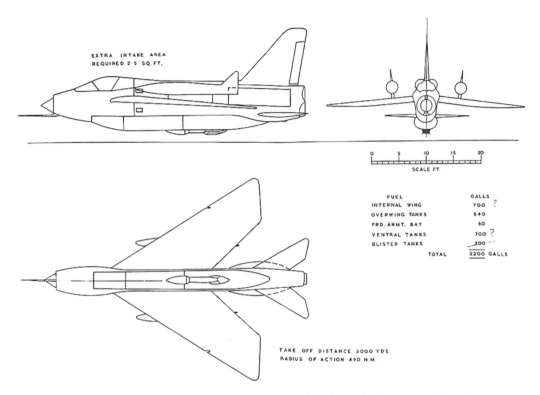

FUEL	GALLS
INTERNAL WING	700 ?
OVERWING TANKS	540
FRD. ARMT. BAY	60
VENTRAL TANKS	700 ?
BLISTER TANKS	200
TOTAL	2200 GALLS

TAKE OFF DISTANCE 3000 YDS.
RADIUS OF ACTION 490 N.M.

Lightning development with RB163 engines and unchanged wing, seen as the only viable configuration from the four considered in the Low Level Strike study, October 28, 1959. Note the single RP3 'Genie' munition proposed for air-to-ground use.

that serious attention be given to the ground attack capability of the Lightning Mk3. At about the same time, EEA received approaches from the Operational Requirements Branch, the Air Ministry and Fighter Command Headquarters on the same subject. These included advice on mission profiles to be studied. In response, on February 3, the company began to prepare a brochure detailing ground attack developments for all marks of Lightning. A copy of the brochure was sent to Pike on March 4. Six copies each were sent to ACAS(OR), AVM Robert Bateson and D(RAF)A, F G R Cook at the Ministry of Aviation.

The brochure described three levels of development. The first applied to Lightning Marks 1, 2 and 4 with AI 23 and the PAS Mk1 aiming system, the second to Marks 3 and 5 with AI 23 and the Light Fighter Sight (LFS). The third introduced further stages of

development of the fire control system suitable for future developments of the Mark 3 and 5 aircraft.

The main focus was on the existing guns and 2in rockets against tactical targets (subsequent discussions suggested that development of a hollow charge head might be necessary to make the rockets effective against an adequate variety of targets). The section on future developments of the Mark 3 and 5 aircraft introduced the revised ventral pack with provision for the carriage of a wider variety of weapons including 1000lb bombs, Zuni rockets, Bullpup missiles or RP3 Genie. Other improvements would include a cambered wing leading edge to improve range and navigation aids to improve accuracy and possibly allow blind attacks.

Copies of the brochure were also sent to Rolls-Royce, Ferranti and Marconi for information and

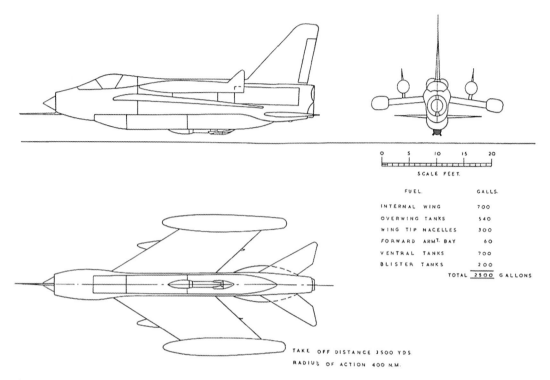

FUEL.	GALLS.
INTERNAL WING	700
OVERWING TANKS	540
WING TIP NACELLES	300
FORWARD ARMᵀ. BAY	60
VENTRAL TANKS	700
BLISTER TANKS	200
TOTAL	2500 GALLONS

TAKE OFF DISTANCE 3500 YDS.
RADIUS OF ACTION 400 N.M.

The most radical layout proposed in the Low Level Strike study – unsurprisingly rejected, October 28, 1959.

comment. Subsequently, a revised version of the brochure was circulated on May 10. This incorporated the latest data on fatigue, weapons and fire control system and included additional analysis of an attack manoeuvre requested by DGARD(RAF), L Boddington, during discussions at Warton in April. In his covering letter, Freddie Page wrote: "We feel that these preliminary studies show that the Lightning can be used satisfactorily in the ground attack role and that comparatively modest development could increase the capability substantially." The firm would be pleased to undertake more detailed studies to a definite operational requirement.

Throughout the remainder of 1960, much of the work focused on the manoeuvre demands of the ground attack role and the resulting fatigue loads on the aircraft structure. The statistical assumptions to be made were a major topic of debate between EEA and RAE. Estimates based on expected manoeuvre patterns showed a big difference compared to real-life

records for existing aircraft such as Venom and Javelin. Eventually the emphasis shifted to real-life records for the Hunter when they became available.

On May 9, 1960, Specification 23/49P3 was issued to cover the production standard of the Lightning Mk3. This introduced ground attack requirements into the clauses about the fire control system. The same applied to Specification T205D&P for the two-seat Mark 5 when it was issued on December 5.

However, on July 19, Roland Beamont reported to Page that in recent conversation with Harold Watkinson MP (Minister of Defence) he had been told that Tom Pike had said that the Lightning was "too sophisticated" for the ground attack role but that he would get Air Commodore Hughes (Air member of the Defence Research Policy Staff) to look into it in case there was any chance of using it. Hughes had subsequently been in touch with Beamont and had asked for the latest written information on the subject.

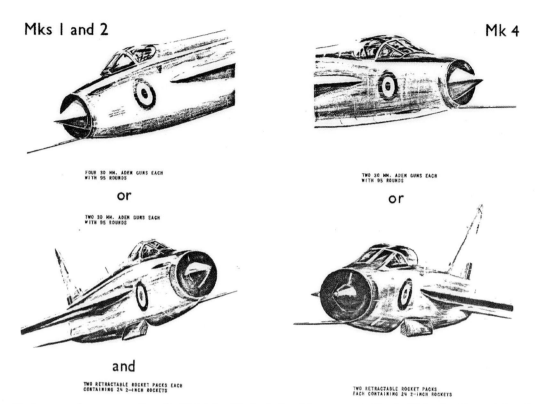

Mks 1 and 2

Mk 4

FOUR 30 MM. ADEN GUNS EACH
WITH 95 ROUNDS

TWO 30 MM. ADEN GUNS EACH
WITH 95 ROUNDS

or

or

TWO 30 MM. ADEN GUNS EACH
WITH 95 ROUNDS

and

TWO RETRACTABLE ROCKET PACKS EACH
CONTAINING 24 2-INCH ROCKETS

TWO RETRACTABLE ROCKET PACKS
EACH CONTAINING 24 2-INCH ROCKETS

Air-to-ground weapon options for Lightning Marks 1, 2 and 4 as presented in the Lightning Ground Attack brochure, March 1960. This is essentially the use of the existing guns and rocket pods against ground targets.

Meanwhile, progress continued to be made in discussions with the Air Ministry and Ministry of Aviation. A review meeting was held on August 30. Development options were discussed under two categories. The first covered minor modifications to allow the use of 2in rockets; the second covered possible further improvements of a basic nature to give the aircraft a full ground attack role. It was suggested that four of the aircraft supplied to CFE for evaluation could be taken back to use as development aircraft for the minor modifications. EEA was to produce estimates of time and cost to modify these aircraft to introduce three features: the ability to select the rocket battery pack, extend flap extension clearance up to 400kts and provide target 'in range' indication. Ferranti would give an indication of the cost of modifying AI 23 to give the 'in range' signal.

The consideration of further developments turned out to be limited. The only new weapon of interest to the Air Staff was the Bullpup missile. EEA outlined the possible carriage locations and the studies and tests that would be needed. The company also pointed out that, given the need to guide the missile via a hand controller, a second crew member might be an advantage. As to improved navigation, adaptation of the existing TACAN equipment was seen as preferable to adding Doppler navigation equipment. Any decision on introducing the cambered wing leading edge was deferred pending more information about its impact on different missions. Equally, a decision about the new ventral pack was deferred until the firm could assess the possibility of retrofitting it to the Mark 1 and 2 aircraft.

In the aftermath of the meeting, EEA pursued contract funding for applying the minor modifications to the CFE aircraft. It was accepted that funding

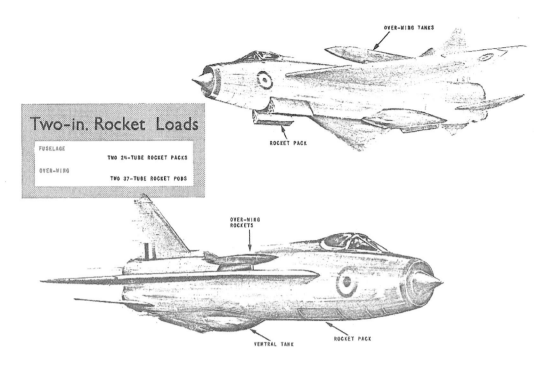

Air-to-ground weapon options for Lightning Marks 3 and 5 as presented in the Lightning Ground Attack brochure, March 1960. This introduces extra overwing rocket pods, raising the total number of rockets from 48 to 122. Overwing fuel tanks are an alternative for longer range missions.

of studies of further developments would be deferred until the next Lightning Policy Board meeting and that consideration of retrofitting the revised ventral pack with RP3 provision would be covered by existing funding for the Mark 2 to Mark 3 conversion study.

However, on September 23 EEA was advised by the RTO that the Finance Board had ruled out any release of funding until specific Ministry of Defence authority was obtained. In fact, Page had already been informed of this at the Management Board meeting on September 15 and it was confirmed by a letter from DGARD(RAF), L Boddington, on September 28. On the same day a letter from RAF/AI stated that, although the development funding had been deferred until submission of an official Air Ministry requirement, the firm was still requested to provide the cost estimate. In reply to Boddington, on September 29, Page confirmed that all work had stopped.

The cost estimate was submitted following confirmation via the RTO on November 2 that no further work was to be undertaken on the ground attack role until an Air Staff Requirement had been stated. On November 23, EEA staff were informed that Page and Atkin had agreed that all facilities specifically for ground attack should be deleted from the Lightning Mark 3 and 5 following MoA instructions that no money should be spent developing Lightning for the ground attack role.

At the System Integration Committee meeting on December 21, however, there was discussion as to whether the ground attack clauses of Specifications 23/49P3 and T205D&P should continue to be met. It was agreed that they should. This was confirmed at the Lightning Management Board meeting on January 13, 1961. At this meeting, Page assured the board that there had been no intention of omitting provision for the 'in range' signal or for the 2in rockets to be fired manually as in the standard air-to-air

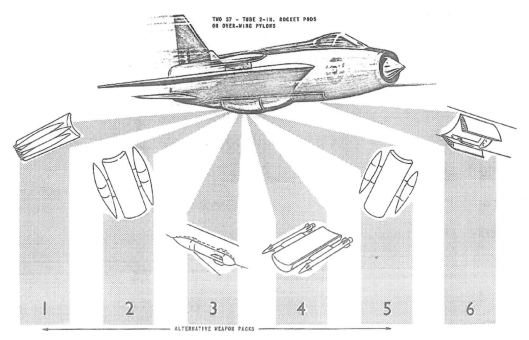

1. 1, 2 OR 3 1,000 LB R.1 BOMBS
2. TWO ZUNI ROCKET PODS ON PYLONS, 4 ROCKETS IN EACH POD
3. ONE R.P.3 ROCKET PROJECTILE

4. TWO BULLPUP MISSILES ON PYLONS
5. TWO 24-TUBE 2-IN. ROCKET PODS ON PYLONS
6. TWO 24-TUBE 2-IN ROCKET PACKS

TWO 37 - TUBE 2-IN. ROCKET PODS
ON OVER-WING PYLONS

ALTERNATIVE WEAPON PACKS

Air-to-ground weapon options for a developed Lightning Mark 3 as presented in the Lightning Ground Attack brochure, March 1960. This introduces the idea of a larger ventral pack with extra fuel and a weapons pack bay with provision for carriage of a much wider range of stores. This had already been mooted in an export context.

role (i.e. without the extra selection facilities originally proposed). Confirmation of this agreement was requested by MoA on January 20 and given by EEA on March 1.

From now on, most new ground attack developments were in the context of developing a multi-role version of the Lightning for export. Studies to this end had been going on since 1958. For the next 18 months, although numerous weapons were considered, there was little detailed technical work.

In early 1962, Bristol Aircraft, now part of British Aircraft Corporation with EEA, Vickers and Hunting, proposed a new air-to-ground missile. An EEA report, dated February 21, looked at its carriage by Canberra, TSR2, Lightning Mark 3 and Mirage IIIv. The Lightning installation used a weapons pack proposed as a substitute for the centre section of the new, larger

ventral tank. Cooling and electrical supplies would come from the existing aircraft systems. The report noted that the carriage of two weapons, one either side of the ventral pack, had already been proposed for Bullpup, Nord AS30 and AS20, 1000lb bombs, pods with thirty-seven 2in rockets, pods with four Zuni rockets and the Matra R530 missile.

Finally, on October 1, 1963, a meeting was held at the RAE to review the large range of air-to-surface weapons that was becoming available in the UK and USA. Following this, attention returned to developing the fire control system.

On December 13, EEA approached Ferranti for advice on the feasibility of modifying AI 23 to provide radar ranging and sighting information, either by direct modification of the basic Lightning installation or possibly by having an interchangeable radar unit.

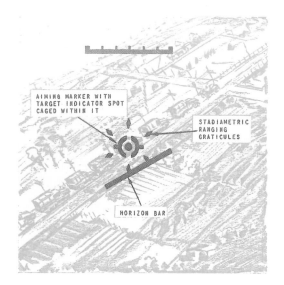

Pilot's Attack Sight (PAS)   Light Fighter Sight (LFS)

Ground attack aiming presentations proposed for different Lightning marks (Pilot's Attack Sight, PAS Mk1, for Lightning Marks 1, 2 and 4; Light Fighter Sight, LFS, for Marks 3 and 5).

This was required for a study of the development of Lightning Marks 1, 1A, 2 and 3 for a ground attack role.

By February 1964, a brochure for a ground attack version of Lightning Mk3 with and without variable geometry wings had been drafted; but this had been put on hold after discussions with the Air Ministry and CFE. More detailed investigation of the sighting and aiming system was required. A meeting was planned to discuss AI 23B and LFS modifications and this was held on February 6.

As well as outlining suitable LFS modifications, Ferranti described the proposed 'PALLAS' system (Pilot Action for Low Level Sight) for ground attack with retarded bombs. While attractive for its accuracy and flexibility (it could also be used in dive attacks), the amount of setting up to be done while flying at low altitude made two-seat operation preferable. It had an expected in-service date of 1968/69.

Following further discussions, on October 8, 1964, what was now the Preston Division of the British Aircraft Corporation placed a contract on Ferranti to design specific modifications to AI 23 for ground attack. The company was also required to manufacture a modification kit and embody this in an AI 23 set to be supplied by BAC Preston. This and development work for under-wing pylons in 1965 finally set in train the development of the Mark 53 export variant of the Lightning.

Following discussions with DOR1, Air Commodore Edgar James, Lightning Project Manager Alec Atkin wrote to him and D(RAF)B, R P Dickinson, on February 23, 1965, about possible Lightning developments. With regard to Strike options he noted that, as a result of work in aid of the Saudi air force, EEA was confident of carrying a fair range of weapons satisfactorily in this role. Use of a two-seat aircraft was advocated. With minor modifications, the AI 23/PAS system was ideal for aiming free-fall weapons, guns and rockets against ground targets—and the airframe fatigue problem was much less than previously thought.

This work for the Royal Saudi Arabian Air Force and other export customers would continue to be the focus for ground attack developments.

Chapter 8

EXPORT PROPOSALS

As Lightning approached entry into service with the RAF, EECo was allowed to start promoting it to selected potential customers abroad.

Initial export interest came from the Federal Republic of Germany (FRG). Following Germany's withdrawal of interest in the development of the Saunders Roe SR177 in January 1958, Minister of Supply Aubrey James offered the P1B as an alternative to FRG Defence Minister, Franz Josef Strauss. A German technical mission had already visited English Electric at Warton in April 1957.

Now a version of the P1B development brochure was rushed out with a German language front cover. On January 29, 1958, the FRG Technical Mission visited Warton for a flight demonstration of the P1B. Nothing came of this however, as Germany opted for the Lockheed F-104 Starfighter.

The first proposal for a specific export variant came in the form of a major 'Tactical Fighter' proposal to Australia in 1960. This introduced a multi-role fit based on the latest F Mk 3 fighter design. It had a large ventral pack with facilities to allow different role fits to be incorporated as and when desired—including fuel tank, sensor, electronics and armament options. The proposal was aimed at satisfying the Australian requirement (OR AIR 34 Iss4) for a single-seat aircraft. It was suggested, however, that the full weapon system capability could be exploited better by a crew of two. A two-seat, multi-role variant based on the Lightning T Mk 5 was proposed and this was given the project number P33.

Although the Australian proposal was not successful, the general design concept was broadened as a suite of configuration options with the label PL1. These were again based on the Lightning T5 and offered short or long ventral packs, both incorporating additional fuel and a bay for weapons or sensors or yet more fuel for ferrying.

In March 1963, a mock-up of the long, multi-role ventral pack was fitted to Lightning XN725. Photographs show it with a mock-up Bullpup air-to-surface missile on a stub pylon on the side of the ventral tank and some alternative stores alongside (1000lb bombs and pods of Zuni rockets). This may relate to the P34 project for a ground attack variant for the RAF.

By the time a proposal was made to Italy's Aeronautica Militare in 1965, a final design for a larger

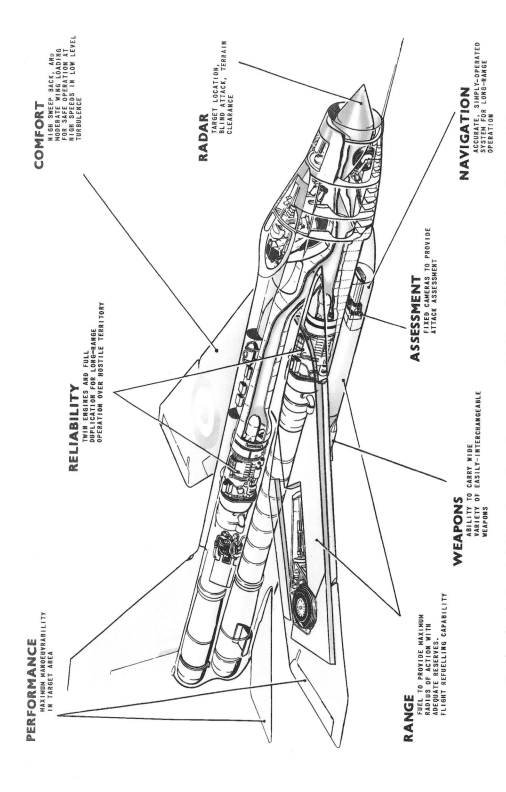

COMFORT

HIGH SWEEP BACK, AND
MODERATE WING LOADING
FOR SAFE OPERATION AT
HIGH SPEEDS IN LOW LEVEL
TURBULENCE

RADAR

TARGET LOCATION,
BLIND ATTACK, TERRAIN
CLEARANCE

NAVIGATION

ACCURATE, SIMPLY-OPERATED
SYSTEM FOR LONG-RANGE
OPERATION

RELIABILITY

TWIN ENGINES AND FULL
DUPLICATION FOR LONG-RANGE
OPERATION OVER HOSTILE TERRITORY

ASSESSMENT

FIXED CAMERAS TO PROVIDE
ATTACK ASSESSMENT

WEAPONS

ABILITY TO CARRY WIDE
VARIETY OF EASILY-INTERCHANGEABLE
WEAPONS

PERFORMANCE

MAXIMUM MANOEUVRABILITY
IN TARGET AREA

RANGE

FUEL TO PROVIDE MAXIMUM
RADIUS OF ACTION WITH
ADEQUATE RESERVES.
FLIGHT REFUELLING CAPABILITY

Developed Lightning Mark 3 in strike configuration as presented in "Australia's Defence" brochure, February 1960.

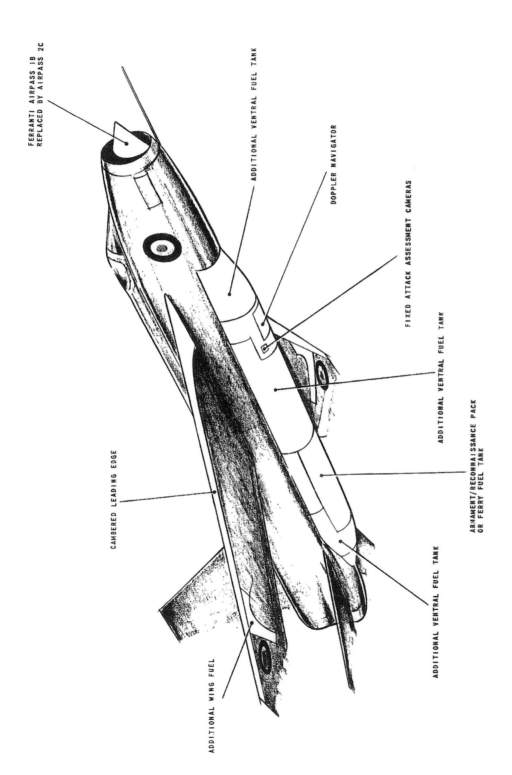

FERRANTI AIRPASS IB
REPLACED BY AIRPASS 2C

ADDITIONAL VENTRAL FUEL TANK

DOPPLER NAVIGATOR

FIXED ATTACK ASSESSMENT CAMERAS

ADDITIONAL VENTRAL FUEL TANK

CAMBERED LEADING EDGE

ARMAMENT/RECONNAISSANCE PACK
OR FERRY FUEL TANK

ADDITIONAL VENTRAL FUEL TANK

ADDITIONAL WING FUEL

Lightning Mark 3 developments proposed to meet the Australian requirement, February 1960.

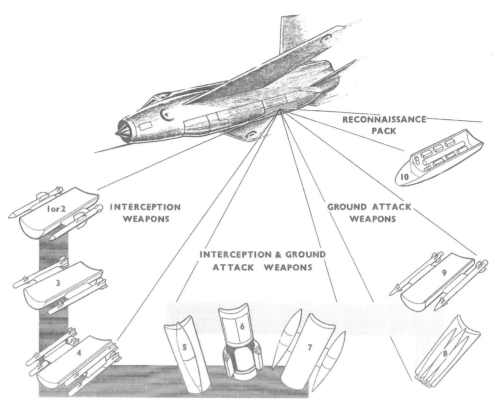

**Armament options presented to Australia, exploiting the weapon
bay in the enlarged ventral pack, February 1960.**

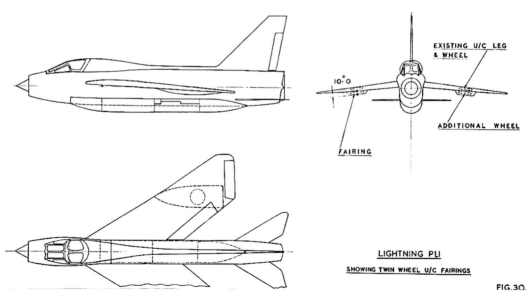

Proposed modification to provide a twin wheel undercarriage for soft field operations, PL1 study, January 1961.

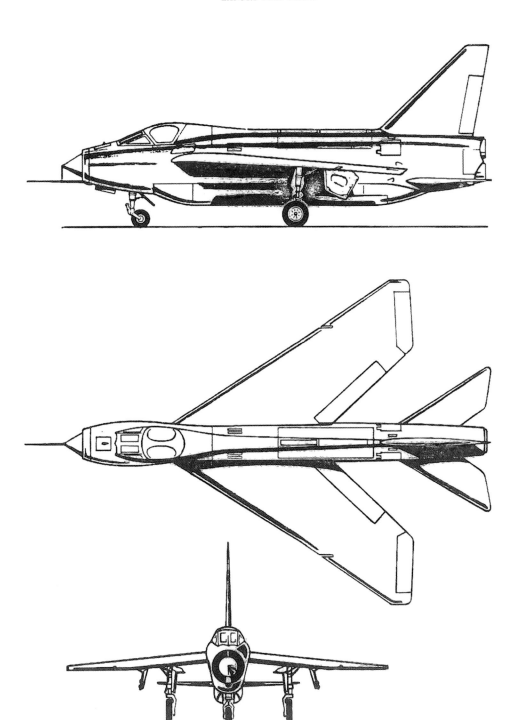

**General arrangement of a developed Lightning Mark 5 suggested
as a better option for Australia, February 1960.**

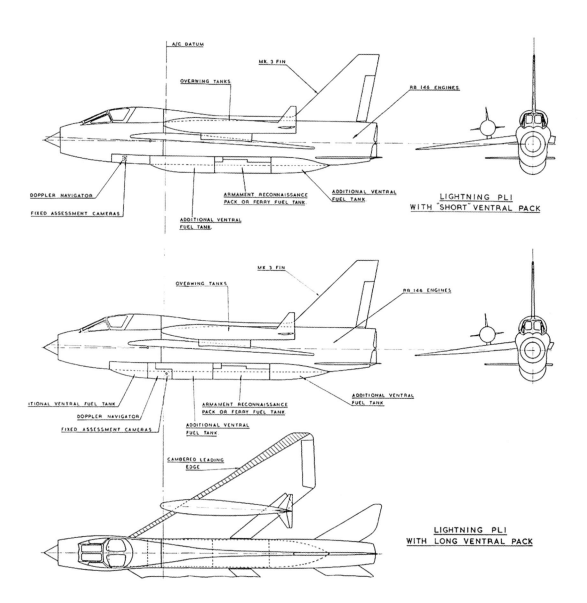

Lightning development options proposed in the PL1 study, January 1961, including short and long versions of the extended ventral pack.

ventral tank was being introduced for RAF Marks F2A, F3A and F6.

This was therefore used as the basis for multi-role export proposals. Possible weapon loads proposed to Italy included a variety of missiles, bombs and rockets. Firestreak, Red Top, 2in rockets pods and the over-wing tanks were classed as existing. Design was proceeding for SNEB rockets and 1000lb bombs. All the remaining items were said to have feasibility established. This design would form the basis for the version eventually exported to Middle Eastern customers as the Mark 53.

A mock-up of the extended ventral pack fitted to Lightning XN725 and showing Bullpup, Zuni rocket pods and 1000lb bombs as potential stores, March 23, 1963.

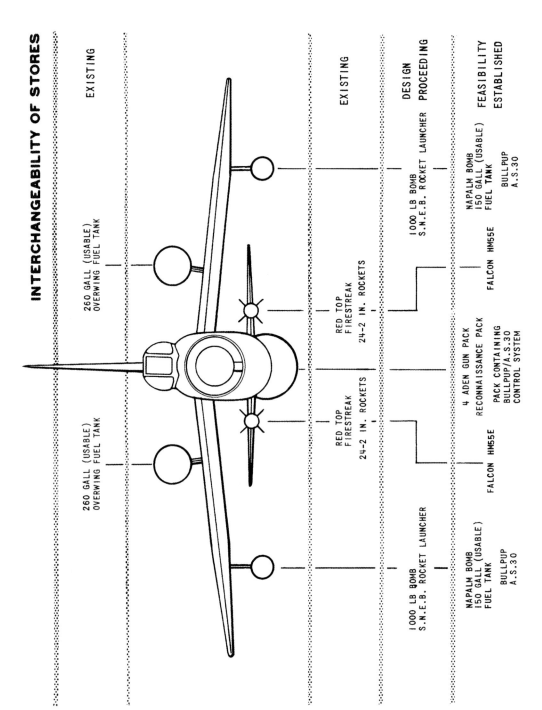

INTERCHANGEABILITY OF STORES

EXISTING

260 GALL (USABLE)
OVERWING FUEL TANK

EXISTING

DESIGN
PROCEEDING

1000 LB BOMB
S.N.E.B. ROCKET LAUNCHER

FEASIBILITY
ESTABLISHED

NAPALM BOMB
150 GALL (USABLE)
FUEL TANK

BULLPUP
A.S.30

FALCON HM55E

RED TOP
FIRESTREAK
24-2 IN. ROCKETS

4 ADEN GUN PACK
RECONNAISSANCE PACK

PACK CONTAINING
BULLPUP/A.S.30
CONTROL SYSTEM

RED TOP
FIRESTREAK
24-2 IN. ROCKETS

FALCON HM55E

NAPALM BOMB
150 GALL (USABLE)
FUEL TANK

BULLPUP
A.S.30

1000 LB BOMB
S.N.E.B. ROCKET LAUNCHER

260 GALL (USABLE)
OVERWING FUEL TANK

Weapon options proposed for Italy, December 1964, broken into three categories: 'existing', 'design in progress' and 'feasible'.

Chapter 9

FIGHTER DEVELOPMENTS

The Defence White Paper of 1957 retained Lightning as the only remaining interceptor project for the RAF and stated that it should be developed to its full capability. Numerous weapon and equipment possibilities were investigated in the period 1957 to 1966. Changing perceptions of air defence requirements and the acceptance of the need for more advanced interceptor types led to the acquisition of the Phantom and then the Air Defence Variant of Tornado. Investment in these eventually over-rode further major investment in the Lightning.

Soon after the first consideration of guided weapon armament for Lightning in 1952, attention had been drawn to air-to-air missile developments in the USA. The Hughes Falcon and its E9a fire control system was considered for RAF use in 1953. By 1955, EECo had gathered details of the various versions of Falcon, Sparrow and the recently developed Sidewinder. At the fifth AI 23 Progress Meeting on June 12, 1956, Ferranti said it had been asked by the MoS to investigate ways of using Sparrow 3 with AI 23 and providing the necessary CW signal. At the sixth progress meeting on October 2, the company reported that it would require either major redesign of the radar

or provision of a separate illuminator.

EECo meetings with US company representatives at the Paris and Farnborough air shows in 1956 produced more details on Falcon and Sidewinder but nothing about intended developments. At this time the MoS was unsupportive of these contacts; although Sparrow was under consideration for carriage on Sea Vixen and possibly F177.

The MoS eventually held a review of alternatives to Blue Jay Mk4 (Blue Vesta) as a replacement for Blue Jay Mk1 (Firestreak) on Lightning in May 1958. It considered four weapons: Sidewinder, Falcon, Sparrow and Genie. Sidewinder was rejected as offering no improvement on Blue Jay Mk1. Falcon offered the attraction of both radar and infra-red guided versions. The radar guided version, however, would require AI radar development to provide target illumination. Furthermore, the infra-red versions offered no coverage improvement over Blue Jay. Finally, the very small warhead made it essentially a 'hittile' and required salvo firing to achieve adequate lethality. American aircraft carried six Falcons for this reason and this would be too difficult for Lightning.

Sparrow was attractive for its radar guidance and

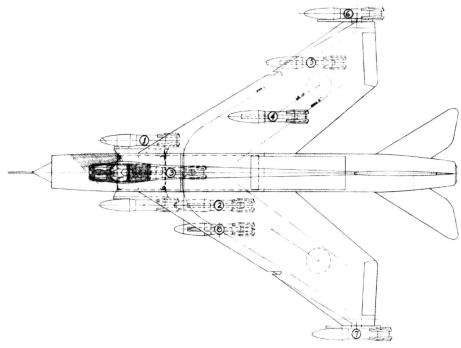

Possible carriage locations explored for Genie, Brochure 42, December 31, 1957.

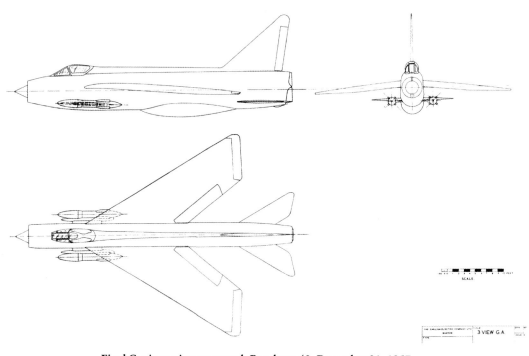

Final Genie carriage proposal, Brochure 42, December 31, 1957.

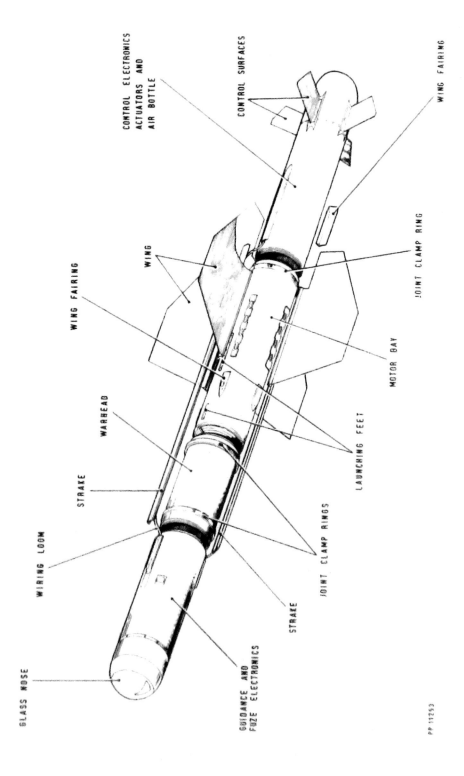

CONTROL ELECTRONICS ACTUATORS AND AIR BOTTLE

CONTROL SURFACES

WING FAIRING

WING

WING FAIRING

JOINT CLAMP RING

WARHEAD

MOTOR BAY

STRAKE

LAUNCHING FEET

WIRING LOOM

JOINT CLAMP RINGS

GLASS NOSE

STRAKE

GUIDANCE AND FUZE ELECTRONICS

PP 11253

Red Top as of de Havilland Propellers Publication 5073, September 1958.

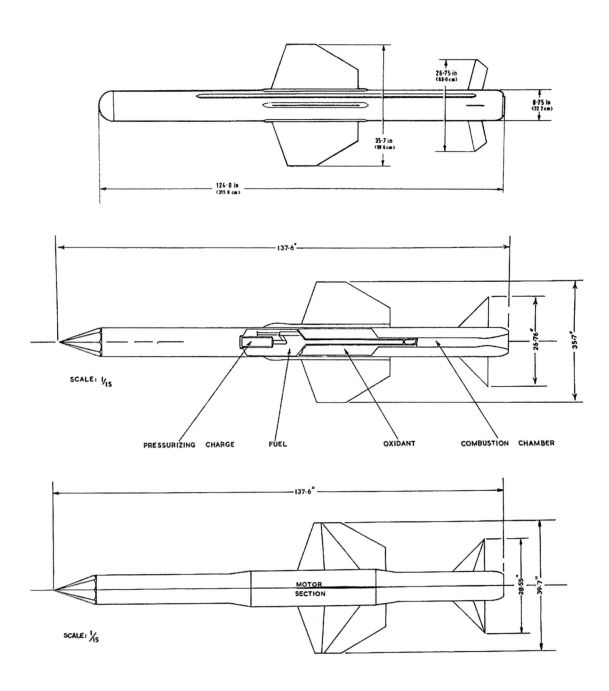

Red Top variants proposed, May 1960. Top: Basic Red Top. Centre: Red Top Mark 2. Bottom: Red Top 'Mark 2 plus' with enlarged boost motor.

hence forward hemisphere capability. It was ruled out, however, because the space could not be found to add the necessary CW illumination. (EECo would later re-examine Sparrow in the context of other radar developments.) This left Genie as the focus for further study since, in spite of its high cost, it seemed to offer a useful increase in engagement capability and simpler integration with the Lightning's systems.

Genie was not a guided missile however; it was an unguided rocket projectile with a 1.5 kiloton nuclear warhead. Its US designation was MB-1 and, from 1963, AIR-2. In the UK it was also known initially as 'Ding Dong' and later as RP3. More than 3000 were produced for US and Canadian deployment in defence of North America. A single live firing test was carried out on July 19, 1957. The warhead was detonated with a yield of about two kilotons 4000 yards after launch and 3000 yards clear of the launch aircraft. The detonation at 18,000ft altitude caused so little radiation at ground level that the weapon was declared safe for use over populated areas.

UK industry had already been tasked with studying the employment of Genie. EECo had studied the carriage and operation of the weapon by Lightning under the project number P23. The study was reported on December 31, 1957. Various carriage locations were explored, finally settling on the standard air-to-air missile position.

The interception profile involved a front hemisphere engagement with the projectile launched on a lofted trajectory. The fighter then broke away in a diving turn to maximise the separation and minimise exposure to blast, heat and radiation. The EECo study was accompanied by a comprehensive weapon study by Ferranti. Work continued into 1959 but by 1960 it was under consideration for cancellation as one of the possible savings during the run-down of Fighter Command. A strong case was made for retaining it for use in defending nuclear forces when deployed to the Far East, but it was finally cancelled by ACAS(OR) on November 4, 1960.

It was now accepted that Red Top offered the only viable way ahead. It had a number of design changes,

including using an indium antimonide (InSb) sensor instead of the lead telluride (PbTe) of Blue Vesta. A brochure detailing the missile characteristics and performance was published in September 1958 followed by a full installation brochure in December 1960. The unit cost was estimated at £12,000–£15,000 compared to £8500 for Firestreak. A stockpile of 2000 Red Tops for the Lightning Mk3 force was considered adequate for the seven days of warfare that might be anticipated in defence of the deterrent.

By 1959, de Havilland had already begun to study improved versions of Red Top. A brochure for Red Top Mk2 was issued in May 1960 (English Electric received a copy on August 15). This proposed replacing the solid fuel 'Linnet' motor with a packaged liquid fuel unit. This could even be fitted as a replacement in existing missiles. It was seen to offer improved shelf life and handling; but the main benefit was a significant increase in thrust to improve the missile-to-target speed ratio.

In the case of the subsonic Sea Vixen, this brought the sizes of the success zones almost up to those achieved by the supersonic Lightning with the basic Red Top. A more radical development proposed a larger diameter motor unit giving even higher missile speeds to provide a big improvement in engaging very high speed targets. For instance, a Mach 0.8 fighter intercepting a manoeuvring Mach 2 target would have a five-fold increase in the success zone.

There was little interest in these proposals for the Lightning. The RAF was in the throes of running down Fighter Command from 400 Hunters and Javelins to 144 Lightnings and finding cost savings such as cancelling Bloodhound Mk3 and the Blue Joker balloon-borne early warning radar while still making the case for 12 squadrons of Lightning Mk3 and Red Top rather than the eight proposed.

However, since the weather limitations of infra-red missile guidance remained a concern, studies continued to explore viable radar guidance options. Continuing from the Blue Jay Mk4 studies, the early Radar Red Top studies looked to GEC to supply the seeker.

The preference was for a CW guidance signal.

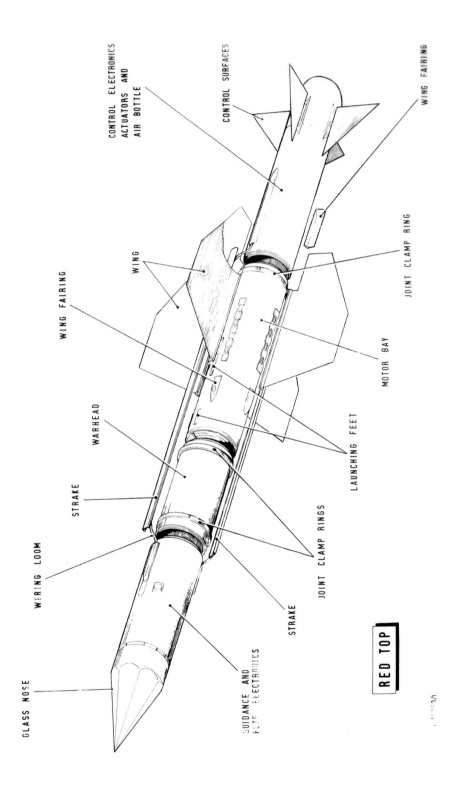

GLASS NOSE

WIRING LOOM

STRAKE

WARHEAD

GUIDANCE AND
FUZE ELECTRONICS

STRAKE

JOINT CLAMP RINGS

WING FAIRING

WING

CONTROL ELECTRONICS
ACTUATORS AND
AIR BOTTLE

CONTROL SURFACES

WING FAIRING

JOINT CLAMP RING

MOTOR BAY

LAUNCHING FEET

RED TOP

Red Top as of de Havilland Guided Weapons Department Installation Brochure Red Top, December 1960.

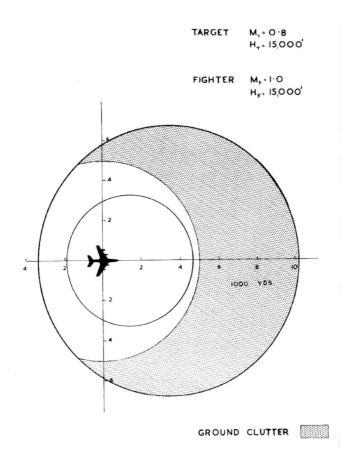

TARGET $M_T = 0.8$
               $H_T = 15,000'$

FIGHTER $M_F = 1.0$
               $H_F = 15,000'$

1000 YDS.

GROUND CLUTTER

A typical launch success zone for Radar Red Top with EMD seeker head as used in Matra 530 (15,000ft altitude, M0.8 target, M1.0 fighter). The shaded area shows the part of the launch zone that would suffer from ground echoes at any range greater than the fighter's altitude.

Furthermore, GEC believed that for various technical reasons a radar guided Red Top was only viable below 45,000ft. These considerations made it more suitable for Sea Vixen with AI 18 rather than Lightning and AI 23. Nevertheless, it was included in a tabular comparison of semi-active radar air-to-air missiles prepared for Ray Creasey on December 12, 1961, which assumed the possibility of either a pulse or CW seeker. Creasey's commentary noted that, since the Navy favoured the CW variant, the cost of developing either a pulse seeker or CW injection for AI 23 would be prohibitive for the Lightning programme. The other missiles considered were Matra 530 with a pulse seeker and the BAC SIG.16 with CW guidance.

Creasey believed that the Matra 530 was the only one suitable for adoption for Lightning.

The 'SIG.16' missile was a Bristol Aircraft concept for an air-to-air derivative of a medium range ship-to-air missile (EEA and Bristol Aircraft were now both part of British Aircraft Corporation). The ship defence missile had been proposed, in competition with designs from EEA Stevenage and Hawker Siddeley, for the UK submission to a NATO requirement.

An EEA appraisal of the air-to-air variant in April 1961 highlighted a number of difficulties. The large booster section would cause severe drag at high speeds and was an obstruction at launch. Provision of the CW illumination would be difficult, although

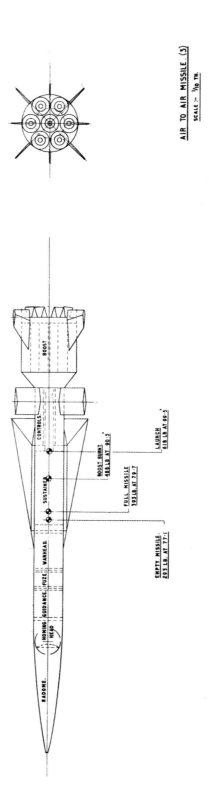

AIR TO AIR MISSILE (3)
SCALE :- 1/10 TH.

BOOST

CONTROLS

SUSTAINER

WARHEAD

FUZE

GUIDANCE

HOMING HEAD

RADOME.

LAUNCH
618 LB. AT 99·5

BOOST BURNT.
488 LB. AT 90·5

FULL MISSILE
593 LB. AT 79·7

EMPTY MISSILE.
293 LB. AT 77·1

Bristol Aircraft proposed air-to-air missile derived from SIG.16 ship-to-air missile study, February 28, 1961.

it might be able to exploit the Q-band ranging radar that was being contemplated (see below). The head-on maximum range, double that of Red Top, was attractive but over-matched the short range of AI 23. In summary, it was difficult to introduce an alternative weapon into a highly integrated system.

A new radar-guided version of Red Top, using the Matra 530 guidance head, was proposed in March 1964. The pulse seeker was compatible with AI 23, but like all simple pulse radars it suffered from ground echo interference at ranges greater than the aircraft's altitude. This was less of a problem at high altitude, but became increasingly significant at medium to low altitudes, exactly where cloud cover necessitated radar homing.

At a meeting of the Lightning Aircraft Systems Integration Committee on November 30, 1963, EEA requested a meeting for guidance on forward thinking and priorities. In response, on February 13, 1964, DOR(A) wrote a summary of desirable developments with regard to performance, weapons and equipment. The focus was on meeting the problems of operating worldwide, given the major changes in the international political situation since Lightning was first designed.

With regard to armament, there was a need to carry secondary armament of guns or rockets as well as Red Top. At the subsequent meeting on March 18, 1964, all of DOR(A)'s topics were addressed together with some additions from EEA including the benefit of variable geometry to meet some of the performance goals. For secondary armament, EEA offered five options:-

A. Aircraft with forward Red Tops plus underwing pylons with gun pods or missiles.

B. Aircraft with an Aden gun installation in the forward bay as per the Mk.1A and Red Tops on underwing pylons.

C. Mk.2A Aircraft with upper guns and Red Top missiles on the forward bay.

D. Aircraft with a mixed load of Red Top and a radar guided Red Top or HM55A Falcon.

E. Aden gun installation in a pack exchangeable with the ventral pack engine hatch tank with the displaced fuel carried in tanks on underwing pylons. These tanks would be jettisoned when empty.

All of the options except A and E were rejected on various grounds of cost, complexity or physical impracticability. Further work was required on the underwing pylons, tanks and gun installations. This led eventually to the choice of the gun installation in the ventral tank.

Sparrow was re-examined in 1965, but this was part of an examination of new target acquisition options which had become the main focus for weapon system improvement.

Two main problem areas were addressed: hostile ECM and the fundamental look-down problems of AI 23 as a basic pulse radar. The ECCM study considered two threats: X-band self-screening jamming of AI 23 or S-band jamming of the GCI link. To counter self-screening jamming, AI 23 had a home-on-jamming mode to give the direction towards the jamming source. This permitted closure until AI burn-through or visual acquisition.

To achieve range information at longer range under these conditions, it was proposed to fit a supplementary Q-band ranging radar. This was studied in detail during 1961. The main problem was finding an installation with adequate field of view. A variety of possible locations were examined. The final choice was to fit it in the front section of the ventral tank. In the end it was not adopted, possibly because of space priorities for other equipment or because of the improved ECCM features of AI 23B.

To cope with S-band Jamming, an S-band homer was proposed. This was developed as a feature of AI 23B and was described in the design notes for the Lightning Mk3 system in May 1960. It went for flight test in 1964 and entered service with the Mark 3.

As a general aid to target acquisition and tracking, especially in severe jamming circumstances,

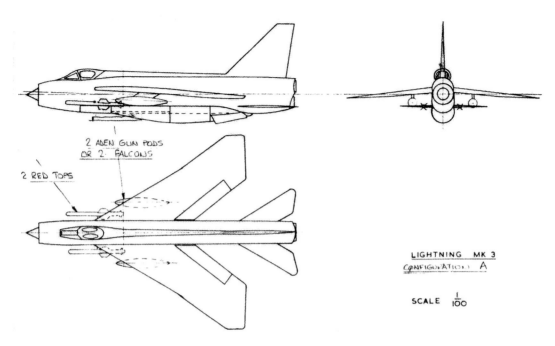

Configuration A as discussed on March 18, 1964: forward Red Tops plus underwing gun pods or missiles.

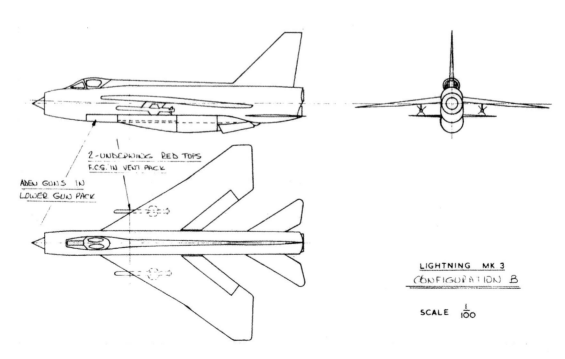

**Configuration B, March 18, 1964: Aden guns in forward bay as
per Mark 1A plus Red Tops on underwing pylons.**

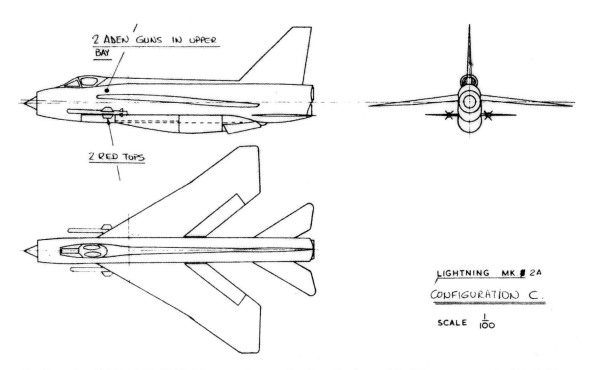

Configuration C, March 18, 1964: Aden guns in upper fuselage plus forward Red Tops as per standard Mark 2A.

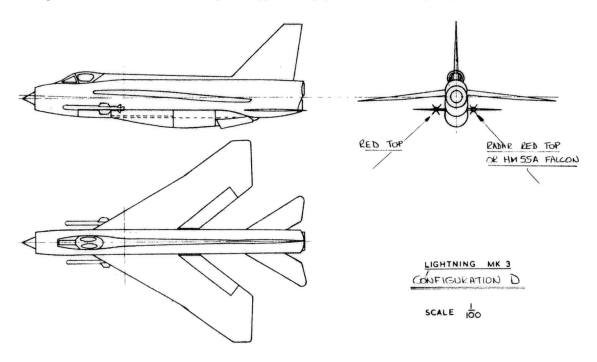

Configuration D, March 18, 1964: Mixed load of Red Top and either a radar guided Red Top or RM55A Falcon.

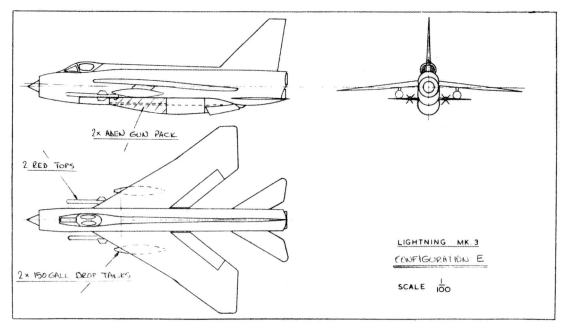

2x ADEN GUN PACK

2 RED TOPS

2x 150 GALL DROP TANKS

LIGHTNING MK 3
CONFIGURATION E

SCALE $\frac{1}{100}$

Configuration E, March 18, 1964: Forward Red Tops plus an Aden gun pack replacing the forward section of the ventral tank with two 150 gal underwing drop tanks.

passive infra-red search and tracking was investigated between 1963 and 1966. Interest focused on the Hughes Aircraft Company 71N Infrared Search and Tracking Set (IRSTS) which was going into service on USAF fighters.

In early 1963, Hughes had approached the UK government and industry proposing the adoption of the IRSTS. EEA had joined them in a high level presentation. By July 22, Hughes was pressing EEA for support in presenting a proposal, jointly with Ferranti, for a trial installation on a Lightning Mk3. The Air Ministry had offered to make a Mk3 available for three months and the MoA had indicated that it could probably obtain funding.

A brief examination suggested that the equipment could be fitted on the upper equipment bay hatch on the nose fuselage. Integration of the IRSTS with AI 23B was considered feasible in discussions with MoA, RRE and Ferranti. More detailed examination was hindered by the current workload of the Warton Electrical Systems Group. Contacts continued, but in January 1964 it was decided that submission of a

brochure would be premature. In February, however, EEA requested the loan of an IRSTS to display at the CFE Convention in April.

A year later, between April and November 1965, RRE trialled an IRSTS installed on a Canberra, but not integrated with a radar. This was then tested against Canberra, Lightning and F-101 targets. In anticipation that the results would confirm the manufacturer's data, Hughes and EEA agreed to review the possible application to Lightning.

EEA would reappraise installation and operation while Hughes would consider redesign to facilitate integration with AI 23B. All of this came to an end when an MoA letter of August 23, 1966, declared that after all due consideration no further information was required.

Two routes were explored to overcome AI 23's look-down limitations: a new Pulse Doppler radar or the addition of Airborne Moving Target Indication (AMTI) to AI 23B. These were also tied to the provision of CW illumination to allow the use of Sparrow III missiles.

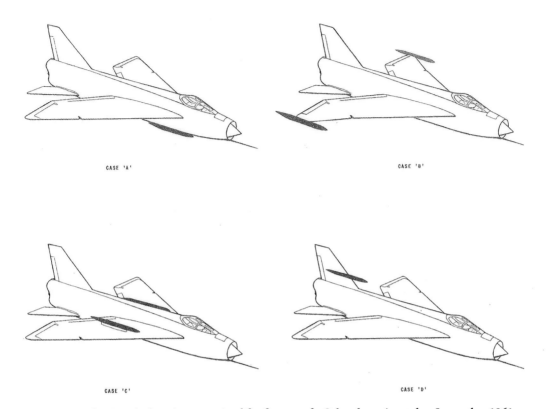

CASE 'A'

CASE 'B'

CASE 'C'

CASE 'D'

Drawings showing the locations examined for fitment of a Q-band ranging radar, September 1961.

On April 8, 1964, a memorandum from Dr J V 'Vic' Hughes to Lightning Project Manager Alec Atkin reported a discussion with EMI and Hughes Aircraft Company (HAC) about a Pulse Doppler radar that they had proposed for P1154 in June 1963. Its functions and features had been outlined and it was clear that its weight of 800lb would be a problem for Lightning. Up to 600lb could be achieved by deleting several functions including range-while-search and track-while-scan. Lowering it to 500–550lb would leave just a basic pulse radar.

This began the search for look-down radar options. During the week that followed, discussions with the RRE confirmed the value of pursuing Pulse Doppler options and a meeting with Westinghouse touched upon radars from the Phantom and radars derived from the Bomarc missile seeker. In July, further information confirmed the Bomarc seeker derivatives being offered for F-104 and F-5A as being most

suitable for Lightning but they were dismissed as not offering enough capability.

Attention turned to Ferranti. Initial interest was in an adaptation of the OSIRIS Pulse Doppler radar being planned for the P1154. It would be re-packaged and have some modes deleted to save weight. This was seen as "pushing the state of the art" and requiring long development.

In September, Elliott Bros wrote to Atkin offering to produce an outline of a radar solution for Lightning within two weeks and a detailed proposal in October. They assumed that a coherent radar would be required in the light of the operational demands on the RAF in Malaysia and Indonesia.

GEC entered the fray in December, offering an MTI module to link to AI 23B. This was under development for AI 18 and being tested on a Canberra. EEA agreed to supply installation ideas and GEC would supply flight test results. EEA offered space

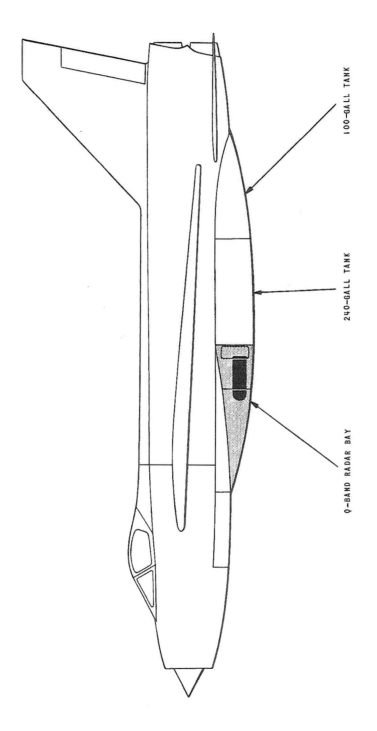

100-GALL TANK

240-GALL TANK

Q-BAND RADAR BAY

Final installation proposal for the Q-band ranging radar, September 1961.

for fitment in the upper nose area.

Through January to March 1965, studies centred on an evolving set of options to be considered with Ferranti to improve the low altitude engagement capability. These were as follows:-

- Replacement of the Light Fighter Sight (LFS) by the Pilot's Attack Sight (PAS)
- Re-packaged OSIRIS radar
- Ferranti coherent AMTI addition to AI 23B
- GEC incoherent AMTI linked to AI 23B
- CW injection into AI 23B for Sparrow III guidance
- A separate CW illuminator slaved to AI 23B

Atkin wrote to D(RAF)B and DOR1 on February 23 to outline ideas for developing Lightning in the interceptor, air superiority fighter, reconnaissance and strike roles. The interceptor options included the spectrum of radars under consideration. The CW provision for Sparrow was linked to the fact that the recent decision to purchase Phantom would bring Sparrow and Sidewinder into the RAF inventory. They could therefore be considered as future primary and secondary armament for Lightning.

By March 16, the OSIRIS development and the Ferranti coherent AMTI module had been dismissed as too expensive to develop. CW injection into AI 23B was also seen as too complex and expensive. Costing therefore focused on PAS, a separate CW illuminator and GEC's incoherent AMTI unit. There were still major reservations about the AMTI especially the difficulty of adapting it to AI 23B with its significant differences from AI 18.

On April 28, 1965, the requirement for Auto-attack was cancelled. This relaxed some of the space restrictions that had hindered the fitting of new equipment.

EMI and HAC then returned with a proposal for a coherent AMTI unit to be integrated with AI 23B. This was CORDS, a system that had been tested as

an addition to the MA1 radar of the F-106 and was expected to be fitted to the APQ-109 pulse radars of some recent Phantoms. A detailed presentation was given on June 10. It was attractive but suffered from a number of deficiencies; in particular there was concern about the multiple blind speeds and the fact that it would prevent the use of the monopulse tracking facility of AI 23B. It would also suffer from the higher sidelobes and lower p.r.f. of AI 23B. Space and environmental limits were problems too.

By September it was felt that there was little hope for it on Lightning. By November, however, more environmentally suitable space had been identified and a programme of phased development trials was suggested. It was still under consideration in December, but space was again proving problematic and the options seemed to be to sacrifice some fuel space in the ventral tank or to delete the S-band homer.

While all these radar studies had been under way, more advanced interceptor projects had been studied against ORs 346, 355 and 356; an interceptor version of TSR2 had been proposed. In January 1964, CFE had produced an outline of requirements for a future fighter, assuming that Lightning Mk.3 would go out of service in the mid-1970s, and a major study of future fighter possibilities had been carried out by industry and the research establishments during 1964 for a committee chaired by Professor R V Jones.

Meanwhile, the Government was grappling with increasing pressures on the defence budget. Everything came to a head with the change of Government in 1964 and the subsequent cancellation of many projects. By 1966, an initial proposal that the RAF's version of the new AFVG should be an interceptor had been dropped in favour of a strike aircraft and the RAF was set to receive the Phantom F4M to OR385. The tightening budget and the priority for funding new aircraft led to the cancellation of the IRST and radar improvements for the Lightning.

Chapter 10

VARIABLE GEOMETRY LIGHTNING

Investigations on the benefits of varying an aircraft's wing sweep in flight began during the Second World War. The idea was then taken further in the USA and UK. At Vickers, between 1945 and 1959, Barnes Wallis pursued the concept to an extreme with his flying-wing designs: Wild Goose and Swallow. Vickers drew upon these studies for its Type 581 in response to OR346/ER206 between 1959 and 1961.

Meanwhile, between 1958 and 1960, NASA had been performing extensive wind tunnel tests on Swallow and other configurations as part of a US/UK joint programme. These revealed that the Swallow's tailless configuration had intractable stability and control problems. The advantages of a swing-wing could be realised best in a conventional tailed design.

Vickers adopted this for subsequent variable geometry (VG) designs such as the Types 583 and 584. To increase confidence in the use of VG for high speed combat aircraft, a research aircraft was suggested—and adaptation of an existing aircraft was seen to be the cheapest route. Vickers initially suggested a swing-wing version of the Swift but this received a lukewarm response. It was felt that, to be useful for future advanced designs, the experimental aircraft should be supersonic. Lightning was the obvious candidate.

Vickers drew up a swing-wing conversion as the Type 588, which was basically a Lightning with new wings. These retained the standard planform when fully swept, but the outer section could be swept forward for low speed flight. By this time, Vickers and English Electric Aviation had been brought together as parts of British Aircraft Corporation.

Warton staff had been alerted to DDOR1's interest in variable geometry at the 1960 SBAC Show. They visited Vickers in April 1961 for a briefing on VG and three months later Vickers turned to BAC Warton for assistance with performance estimates for the Type 588.

Warton began to supply data but pointed out that the low-speed, 25° sweep configuration required experimental evidence for confidence. They had begun to modify a wind tunnel model accordingly. On July 21, Vickers placed a subcontract on Warton to modify an existing Lightning wind tunnel model for tests on the low speed configuration of the Type 588. This was delivered to Vickers in September and some tests were carried out.

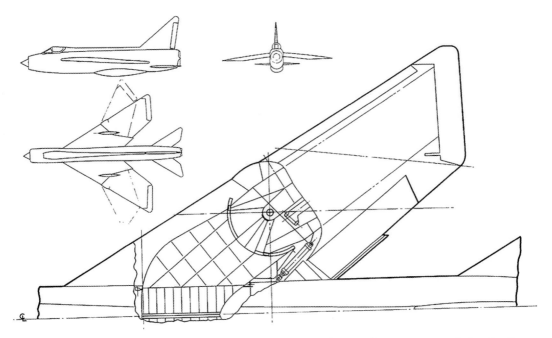

Vickers Type 588 variable geometry research aircraft proposal, general arrangement and wing detail.

Meanwhile, on August 11, CA Sir George Gardner had written to Sir George Edwards at Vickers expressing interest in the work and requesting a copy of Vickers' preliminary estimates of the likely benefits of VG ahead of the confirmatory wind tunnel work. Edwards replied on August 24 with tabulated figures plus a request to spend up to £50,000 from existing project funding on the Lightning work — and proposing further funding to modify two Lightning development batch aircraft to variable sweep.

Gardner's reply on September 12 ruled out the proposed spend and deferred a decision on the way ahead. In November, Warton carried out its own wind tunnel tests and produced a report with both the Vickers and Warton results. No further work seems to have been done for nearly two years.

BAC Warton revived the concept in June 1963 as a possible quick and economical approach to meeting the Royal Navy requirement AW406 for a carrier-based fighter. It drew upon the Vickers work already reported to the Ministry of Aviation and proposed a design based on the Lightning T Mk5

with a new wing as designed by Vickers.

Apart from the VG wing, the main changes were an extended ventral pack, arrestor hook, tail skid, fuselage strengthening, inward retracting undercarriage, dorsal fin and fitment of observer's displays in the starboard crew station. The extended ventral pack was divided into three fuel tanks. The centre tank could be removed and replaced by packs for reconnaissance or ground attack or extra air-to-air missiles or the electronics and aerials for the AST1168 missile. Pylons under the fixed part of the wing could also carry air-to-air or air-to-ground weapons.

The brochure offered a wide variety of weapons. The basic design, adapted from the T Mk5 was shown to meet almost all of the requirements of AW406. It was noted that there would be a small reduction in top speed when carrying four Red Tops instead of the Lightning's usual two. The main deficiencies, however, were due to the limitations of the AI 23B radar. The detection range against a Canberra-type target was 25nm as against the over 60nm required. It could not detect targets flying at low altitude nor

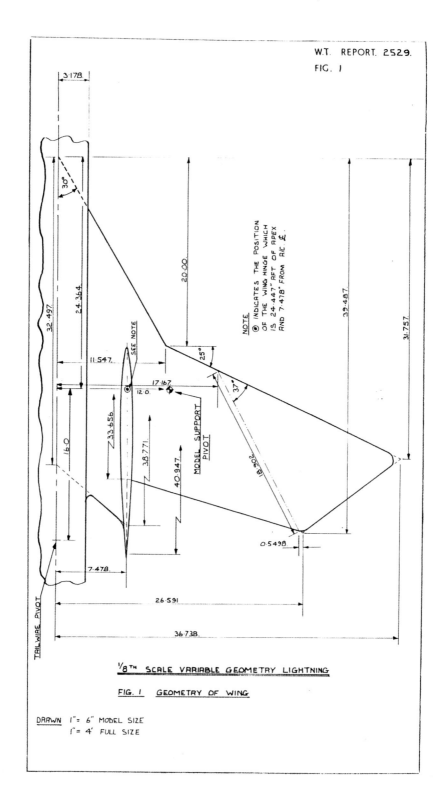

W.T. REPORT. 2529.
FIG. 1

NOTE
⊕ INDICATES THE POSITION OF THE WING HINGE WHICH IS 24·447" AFT OF APEX AND 7·478" FROM A/C ₵.

MODEL SUPPORT PIVOT

TAIL WIRE PIVOT

SEE NOTE

⅛ᵀᴴ SCALE VARIABLE GEOMETRY LIGHTNING

FIG. 1   GEOMETRY OF WING

DRAWN 1" = 6" MODEL SIZE
        1" = 4' FULL SIZE

Geometry drawing of a wind tunnel model for the wing of the Vickers Type 588 tested by Vickers Armstrong, October 1961.

Artist's impression of a navalised Lightning Mark 5 approaching for an arrested landing, "Lightning for the Royal Navy" brochure, June 1963.

provide terrain warning in the ground attack role.

A number of further developments were offered to overcome these deficiencies and increase the overall capabilities. Convergent-divergent nozzles would restore the top speed and weapon carriage could be improved. A change from Avon 301 to RB168 engines would enhance the mission performance but would require a new rear fuselage. The most significant change proposed was the design of an entirely new nose section to accommodate a new radar with a 30in dish. This would necessitate a change to side intakes to provide space for the larger nose with sufficient volume.

This design was presented in more detail in a subsequent brochure titled 'Lightning for the Royal Navy Phase III Developments'. Most of this is devoted to a comparison of performance with alternative new engines, the RB153/61C or the RB168/1R. The former had the advantage of being small enough to fit the existing fuselage. It could also provide performance

to meet AW406 to the letter. On the other hand the RB168, although requiring a larger fuselage, showed significant advantages when considering the performance in more detail and in a wider range of climates.

In the end, nothing came of this. Naval interest was very much focused on the P1154 and then switched to the F-4 Phantom. RAF interest in a VG Lightning lingered on however. In response to a BAC Weybridge query about the Variable Geometry Lightning Mk3, on February 3, 1964, the Lightning Project Office at Warton supplied a draft brochure on a ground attack version with and without VG wings. It was noted that, following discussions with the Air Ministry and CFE, further thoughts were being considered prior to the publication of the final brochure.

A paper by DOR(A) Ernest James of February 13, 1964, listing areas for development, was forwarded to Alec Atkin on February 21 and provided an opportunity to present the range and duration improvement resulting from fitting a VG wing to the Mk3.

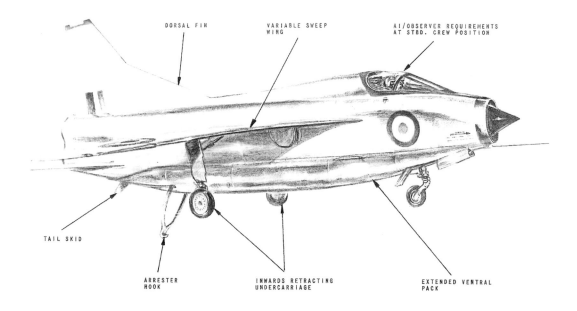

DORSAL FIN

VARIABLE SWEEP
WING

AI/OBSERVER REQUIREMENTS
AT STBD. CREW POSITION

TAIL SKID

ARRESTER
HOOK

INWARDS RETRACTING
UNDERCARRIAGE

EXTENDED VENTRAL
PACK

Changes proposed to navalise the Lightning Mark 5, June 1963.

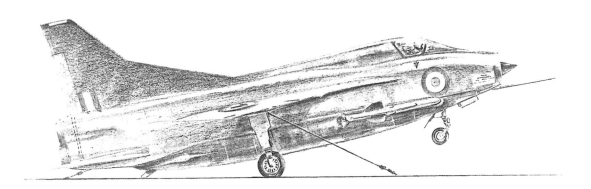

Navalised Lightning Mk5 in take-off attitude, June 1963.

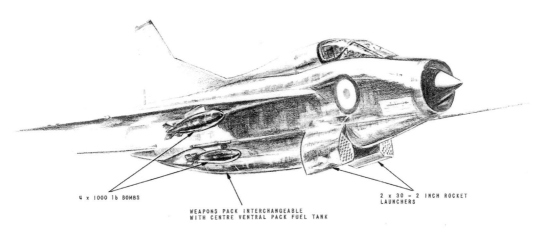

4 x 1000 lb BOMBS

WEAPONS PACK INTERCHANGEABLE
WITH CENTRE VENTRAL PACK FUEL TANK

2 x 30 - 2 INCH ROCKET
LAUNCHERS

Weapon carriage on the navalised Lightning Mk5, June 1963.

Artist's impression of a 'Phase III' navalised Lightning with a revised nose design to accommodate the larger radar necessary to meet Requirement AW406.

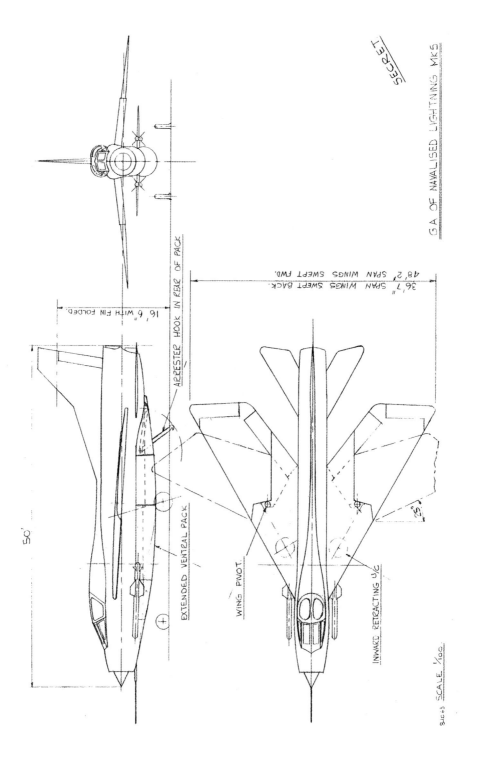

SECRET

GA OF NAVALISED LIGHTNING MK5

48'2" SPAN WINGS SWEPT FWD.

36'7" SPAN WINGS SWEPT BACK.

16'6" WITH FIN FOLDED.

ARRESTER HOOK IN REAR OF PACK

EXTENDED VENTRAL PACK

WING PIVOT.

INWARD RETRACTING U/C

50'

25°

SCALE 1/100

General arrangement of a navalised Lightning Mark 5, October 8, 1963.

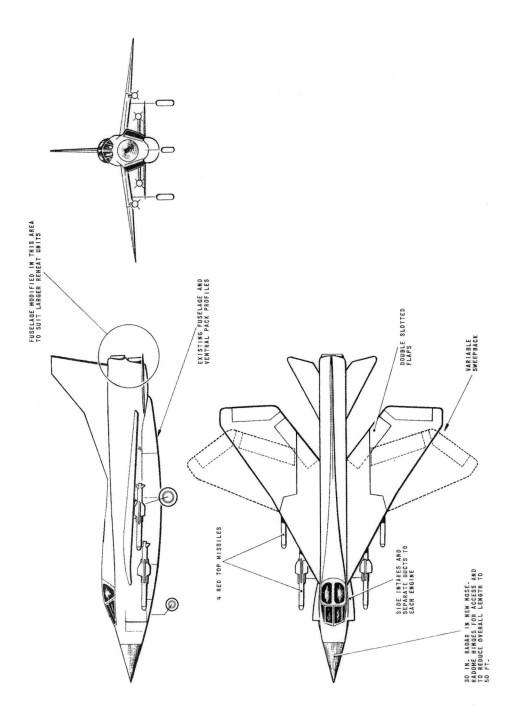

FUSELAGE MODIFIED IN THIS AREA
TO SUIT LARGER REHEAT UNITS

EXISTING FUSELAGE AND
VENTRAL PACK PROFILES

DOUBLE SLOTTED
FLAPS

VARIABLE
SWEEPBACK

4 RED TOP MISSILES

SIDE INTAKES AND
SEPARATE DUCTS TO
EACH ENGINE

30 IN. RADAR IN NEW NOSE,
RADOME HINGES FOR ACCESS AND
TO REDUCE OVERALL LENGTH TO
50 FT.

General arrangement of aircraft with RB153-61C engines, undated brochure "Lightning for the Royal Navy Phase III Developments".

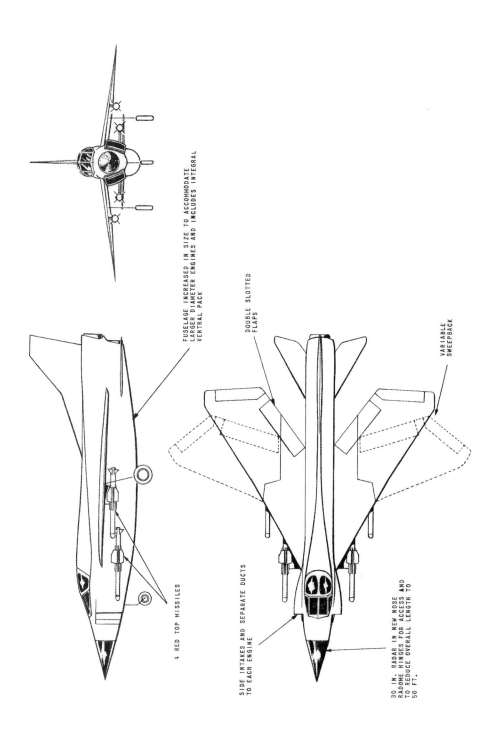

FUSELAGE INCREASED IN SIZE TO ACCOMMODATE
LARGER DIAMETER ENGINES AND INCLUDES INTEGRAL
VENTRAL PACK

DOUBLE SLOTTED
FLAPS

VARIABLE
SWEEPBACK

4 RED TOP MISSILES

SIDE INTAKES AND SEPARATE DUCTS
TO EACH ENGINE

30 IN. RADAR IN NEW NOSE
RADOME HINGES FOR ACCESS AND
TO REDUCE OVERALL LENGTH TO
50 FT.

General arrangement of aircraft with RB168-1R engines, undated brochure "Lightning for the Royal Navy Phase III Developments".

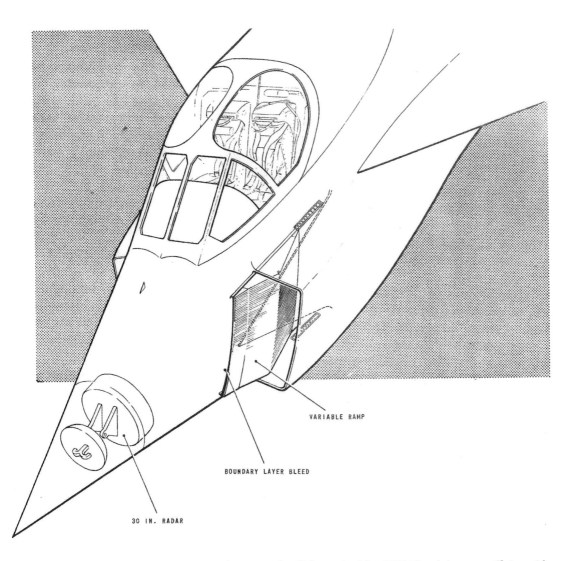

VARIABLE RAMP

BOUNDARY LAYER BLEED

30 IN. RADAR

Detail of the Phase III nose area showing the 30in radar dish required for AW406 and the more efficient side intakes with variable ramps, undated brochure "Lightning for the Royal Navy Phase III Developments".

These were briefed at the meeting on March 18. On April 4, "since considerable interest is being shown by the Ministry and RAF", the firm held a meeting to define a programme of work for a feasibility study. The goal was to achieve a ferry range of 2000nm and operation at maximum all up weight from 2000 yard runways while retaining all the existing high-speed fighter performance.

The wing design would be compatible with the existing fixed wing so that it could be fitted as a conversion. The goal was to retrofit 40 in-service Mk3 aircraft four years after ITP with a target maximum cost of £8.5m for the whole programme. As well as being variable geometry, the new wing was to have increased area and fuel volume. A new wind tunnel model would test the design and a preliminary cost estimate arrived at £6.5m-£7.5m for the development programme, including three prototypes adapted from existing aircraft.

Following a visit to Warton, Group Captain John Ellacombe of the Central Fighter Establishment requested the loan of a slide on the VG Mk3 to use in a presentation on the Mk3 at a forthcoming convention. In supplying it, Lightning Project Manager Alec Atkin stressed the need for a feasibility study to give confidence to the performance estimates and requested CFE's support.

After the convention, on April 24, Air Commodore Ernest Tacon, Commandant of CFE, wrote to Freddie Page expressing thanks for the firm's support. He had taken the opportunity to promote the VG Lightning to C-in-C Fighter Command, VCAS and DCAS. They were all interested, particularly in light of concerns expressed at the convention about the Lightning's lack of range for overseas deployment. Both they and Professor Jones were, however, sceptical of the cost and timescale. Page replied,

summarising the studies to date and pressing again for a feasibility study as being essential for assessing cost and timescale.

A detailed cost estimate on June 15 quoted £4.8m for development, including two prototypes, and £6m for modification of 40 aircraft leading to a cost without profit of £10.8m.

At about this time the project seems to have been dropped, possibly because of the change of Government or because the application of variable geometry was being focused on new aircraft designs.

For these same reasons, over the next two years, all of the major development studies for the RAF's Lightning were wound up. For the RAF at this time, the main debate centred on procuring the existing design in appropriate numbers. Multi-role capability would evolve only for the export Marks. During the long service life ahead, developments would be limited to items essential to achieve and maintain the full capability of the original weapon system in the Mark 3 and, eventually, the Mark 6.

Notes and References

ABBREVIATIONS

AAM	Air-to-Air Missile		BAC	British Aircraft Corporation
A&AEE	Aeroplane and Armament Experimental Establishment		CA	Controller Aircraft
			CAS	Chief of the Air Staff
ACAS	Assistant Chief of the Air Staff		CFE	Central Fighter Establishment
ACM	Air Chief Marshal		CGWE	Controller Guided Weapons and Electronics
ADC	Advisory Design Conference			
ADV	Air Defence Variant (of Tornado)		CORDS	Coherent On Receive Doppler System
AFVG	Anglo-French Variable Geometry (aircraft)		CS(A)	Controller of Supplies (Air)
			CVD	Co-ordination of Valve Development Department
AI	Air Intercept (radar)			
AM	Air Marshal		CW	Continuous Wave
AMTI	Airborne Moving Target Indication		D(RAF)A	Director RAF Aircraft Research and Development (A)
AUS	Assistant Under Secretary		D(RAF)B	Director RAF Aircraft Research and Development (B)
AUW	All Up Weight			
AVM	Air Vice Marshal		DCAS	Deputy Chief of the Air Staff
AW	Armstrong Whitworth		DDOR	Deputy Director of Operational Requirements

DGAP	Director General of Aircraft Production		MTI	Moving Target Indication
DGARD(RAF)	Director General of Aircraft Research and Development (Royal Air Force)		NACA	National Advisory Committee for Aeronautics
DGTD	Director General of Technical Development		NASA	National Air & Space Administration
DMARD	Director of Military Aircraft Research and Development		OR	Operational Requirement
			OSD	Out of service date
DOR	Director of Operational Requirements		p.r.f.	Pulse repetition frequency
DRPC	Defence Research Policy Committee		PAS	Pilot Attack Sight
			PDSR(A)	Principal Director of Scientific Research (Air)
DSRD	Director of Servicing Research and Development		R&D	Research and development
ECCM	Electronic Counter-Countermeasures		RAE	Royal Aircraft Establishment
			RAF	Royal Air Force
ECM	Electronic Countermeasures		RDQ(F)	Research Development Equipment Installation (Fighter Command)
EEA	English Electric Aviation			
EECo	English Electric Company		RN	Royal Navy
EMD	Electronique Marcel Dassault		RRE	Royal Radar Establishment
FAA	Fleet Air Arm		RTO	Resident Technical Officer
FIS	Future Identification System		SAGW	Surface-to-Air Guided Weapon
FRG	Federal Republic of Germany		SAM	Surface-to-Air Missile
GCI	Ground-controlled Intercept		SBAC	Society of British Aircraft Constructors
GEC	General Electric Company			
HAC	Hughes Aircraft Company		SIF	Selective Identification Feature
IFF	Identification Friend or Foe		SNEB	Société Nouvelle des établissements Edgar Brandt
IRSTS	Infra-red Search and Track Set			
ITP	Intention To Proceed		TACAN	Tactical Air Navigation (system)
LFS	Light Fighter Sight			
MAP	Ministry of Aircraft Production		TI	Trial Installation
MoA	Ministry of Aviation		TRE	Telecommunications Research Establishment
MoS	Ministry of Supply		USAF	United States Air Force
MRAF	Marshal of the Royal Air Force		VCAS	Vice Chief of the Air Staff
			VG	Variable Geometry

SOURCES

1. BAE Systems Warton Heritage:-

Drawing Archive

EAG Drawing Register

Freddie Page Archive: FWP 1-1_22f, FWP 4-1_7, FWP 4-1_17, FWP 4-1_18, FWP 4-1_28, FWP 4-3_LA033, FWP 4-3_LA036, FWP 5-3_59, FWP 6-2_10, FWP 6-2_11, FWP 7-2_5/9, FWP 9-4_P1

Main Document Archive: Boxes HA268, HA413, HA765, HA913, HA964, HA1076, HA1080, HA1135, HA2521, HA2523, HA2525, HA2530, HA2531, HA2533, HA2543, HA2548, HA7047, HA7050, HA7395, HA7449 and uncatalogued Wind Tunnel records

F W Page, Memoirs (unpublished)

Gloster Co. Board Reports

R F Creasey, Propulsion/Aircraft Design Matching Experience, AGARD Lecture Series No. 65, 1973

K Emslie, The Wind Tunnel Department at Warton Aerodrome, BAE Systems Heritage Dept., 2010

2. The National Archives (TNA);-

ADM 1/25429, AIR 2/12686, AIR 2/13059, AIR 2/13267, AIR 2/13554, AIR 2/14963, AIR 2/14965, AIR 2/16522, AIR 2/16533, AIR 6/110, AIR 8/1641, AIR 19/937, AIR 20/6721, AIR 20/7395, AIR 20/8594, AIR 20/8596, AIR 20/8598, AIR 20/11481, AVIA 6/17937, AVIA 6/19287, AVIA 13/664, AVIA 13/1327, AVIA 53/14, AVIA 54/419, AVIA 54/427, AVIA 54/2258, AVIA 65/93, AVIA 65/94, AVIA 65/273, AVIA 65/1274, AVIA 65/1275, AVIA 65/1407, AVIA 65/1769, DEFE 7/2062, DEFE 8/46, T 225/1401

3. Miscellaneous Sources

E C Polhamus & T A Toll, *Research Related to Variable Sweep Aircraft Development,* NASA TM 83121, 1981

C Maag & J Ponton, *Shots Diablo to Franklin Prime. The Mid-series Tests of the Plumbob Series, 15 July – 30 August 1957,* DNA 6006F, 1981

Report of RAE Advanced Fighter Project Group, RAE Report Aero 2300, November 1948.

ACKNOWLEDGEMENTS

This book had its origins in two papers delivered on behalf of BAE Systems Heritage to a Royal Air Force Historical Society seminar on the Lightning at the RAF Museum Hendon on 3 October 2018 and published in the society's Journal 72. I am grateful to RAF Historical Society and BAE Systems Heritage for their support and encouragement for the development of the book. Many thanks also to Tony Buttler, Denis Calvert, Chris Gibson and Dan Sharp for their generous sharing of research material. Special thanks also of course to my wife, Liz, for her support, encouragement, patience and sound advice.

For more about the RAF Historical Society and BAE Systems Heritage, see the following internet pages:-

https://www.rafmuseum.org.uk/research/default/raf-historical-society-journals.aspx

and https://www.baesystems.com/en/our-company/heritage

Annex 1

'LIGHTNING' PROJECTS

Project Number	Description
P1	Fighter/Transonic Research Aircraft
P1A	Day fighter
P1B	Day/night fighter
P3	P1 development with side intakes
P5	P1 developments with single RA12 engine and 2000K reheat
P6	Mach 2 Research Aircraft to Spec ER134T
P8	High Altitude Fighter to Spec F155T
P11	P1B Two-seater Trainer Variant to OR318 (Became Lightning T4)
P15	P1B Photo Reconnaissance Version
P18	P1B Tactical Bomber Variant
P19	P1B-Interceptor Development with RB133 engines
P23	Installation of Genie on Lightning
P25	Lightning Mk2 for RAF
P26	Lightning Mk3 for RAF
P27	Lightning Mk5 for RAF
P33	Lightning 2 seat strike fighter to Australian OR AIR 34 (Issue 4)
P34	Lightning Ground Attack Single Seat Aircraft for the RAF

Index